OpenStack Cloud Security

Build a secure OpenStack cloud to withstand all
common attacks

Fabio Alessandro Locati

BIRMINGHAM - MUMBAI

OpenStack Cloud Security

First published: July 2015

Production reference: 1220715

Published by Packt Publishing Ltd.
Livery Place
35 Livery Street
Birmingham B3 2PB, UK.

ISBN 978-1-78217-098-3

www.packtpub.com

Credits

Author
Fabio Alessandro Locati

Reviewers
Pedro Navarro Pérez
Vinoth Kumar Selvaraj

Commissioning Editor
Kartikey Pandey

Acquisition Editor
Nikhil Karkal

Content Development Editor
Mamata Walkar

Technical Editor
Namrata Patil

Copy Editors
Puja Lalwani
Laxmi Subramanian

Project Coordinator
Sanjeet Rao

Proofreader
Safis Editing

Indexer
Tejal Soni

Graphics
Jason Monteiro

Production Coordinator
Melwyn D'sa

Cover Work
Melwyn D'sa

About the Author

Fabio Alessandro Locati is an Italian IT external consultant. His main areas of expertise are Linux, networking, security, data centers, and OpenStack. With more than 10 years of working experience in this field, he has experienced different IT roles, technologies, and languages. Fabio has worked for many different companies, starting from a one-man company to huge companies such as Tech Data and Samsung. This has allowed him to consider various technologies from different points of view, helping him develop critical thinking and understand whether a particular technology is the correct one in a very short span of time.

Since he is always looking for better technologies, he also tries new technologies to see their advantages over the old ones. Two of the most important things Fabio evaluates in a technology are its internal security and the possibility of additional security through configuration or interaction with the other technologies. For virtualization, he often uses OpenStack due to its power and simplicity, ever since he first tried it in 2011. Fabio has used OpenStack for the public-facing cloud, as well as the internal clouds.

I would like to thank my parents, who introduced me to computer science before I was even able to write, and my whole family, who has always been supportive.

A special thanks goes to everyone I worked with at Packt Publishing for their hard work and to the reviewers for their constructive feedback.

Of course, I would also like to thank NASA, Rackspace, the OpenStack community, and all the companies that have created and improved OpenStack over the years.

About the Reviewers

Pedro Navarro Pérez works as an OpenStack specialist at Red Hat. He does training, coding, configuration, and installation of OpenStack; he is also a major contributor to OpenStack on Hyper-V.

Prior to working for Red Hat, Pedro spent several years working as a developer for award-winning cloud start-ups. Pedro graduated from Telecom Bretagne and Universidad Politécnica de Valencia in 2008.

He also likes salsa, playing handball, and evangelizing about how to cook authentic Valencian paella. He currently resides in Barcelona, Spain.

Vinoth Kumar Selvaraj is an enthusiastic computer science engineer from Tamil Nadu, India. He works as an OpenStack engineer for Cloudenablers. He is a graduate from Sri Ram Engineering College, Veppampattu, Chennai. He has been working on various cloud-based technologies and their integrations since the beginning of his career. He is constantly striving to learn new technologies and learn better and faster ways to solve problems.

He is an active member of the OpenStack community at `https://ask.openstack.org/en/users/1825/vinoth/`.

In his spare time, Vinoth enjoys sharing his insights on technologies at `http://www.hellovinoth.com` and via his Twitter handle `@vinoth6664`.

I wish I could thank everyone personally, but let me thank Amma, Appa, Anna, and my friends for their love and support.

I would also like to thank Konda Chendil, Rathinasabapathy, Thiruvalluvar, Venkatesh Perumal, and Krishna Kumar for their support and trust in me.

www.PacktPub.com

Support files, eBooks, discount offers, and more

For support files and downloads related to your book, please visit www.PacktPub.com.

Did you know that Packt offers eBook versions of every book published, with PDF and ePub files available? You can upgrade to the eBook version at www.PacktPub.com and as a print book customer, you are entitled to a discount on the eBook copy. Get in touch with us at service@packtpub.com for more details.

At www.PacktPub.com, you can also read a collection of free technical articles, sign up for a range of free newsletters and receive exclusive discounts and offers on Packt books and eBooks.

https://www2.packtpub.com/books/subscription/packtlib

Do you need instant solutions to your IT questions? PacktLib is Packt's online digital book library. Here, you can search, access, and read Packt's entire library of books.

Why subscribe?

- Fully searchable across every book published by Packt
- Copy and paste, print, and bookmark content
- On demand and accessible via a web browser

Free access for Packt account holders

If you have an account with Packt at www.PacktPub.com, you can use this to access PacktLib today and view 9 entirely free books. Simply use your login credentials for immediate access.

Table of Contents

Preface

As our society moves from an analog world to a digital world, it is easier for ill-intentioned people to attack privates, companies, banks, and government for their advantage or for the other party's damage. Since the beginning of information technologies, we have seen a shift to digitalize our world, and this process has been accelerating ever since. The virtualization has concentrated more data on even less systems, making these systems very nice targets for attacks. Making the clouds secure will be one of the biggest security challenges for the next 10 years, from my point of view. The goal of this book is to prepare cloud administrators for this challenge.

The structure of this book is designed to give you a wide perspective on security. This has multiple reasons. First of all, programs change, but a secure mindset is often more important than knowing how to secure a very specific software, also because very often people specialize in a particular part of the IT sector and kind of lose track of what there is around the technology they master. This often leads to huge security problems in between the areas of expertise of the various people of the team.

OpenStack allows very powerful infrastructures, but tends to be pretty complex, being a solution to many different situations, making it, often, very interesting from a business point of view, but very hard to manage safely.

What this book covers

Chapter 1, First Things First – Creating a Safe Environment, teaches you about a lot of basic security concepts. Also, you'll see a lot of things to be kept in mind while designing a data center as well as new security policies.

Chapter 2, OpenStack Security Challenges, allows you to discover the different kinds of clouds and how this affects security and also the possible types of attacks. In the second part of the chapter, you'll see the various parts of OpenStack and what they do.

Chapter 3, *Securing OpenStack Networking*, shows you how the OSI networking model works from a security perspective and a lot of possible network attacks for each OSI level. In the second part of the chapter, you can see how to harden OpenStack and a few utilities OpenStack networking can provide to make your workflow more secure.

Chapter 4, *Securing OpenStack Communications and Its API*, explains how the encryption works in our world, and, therefore, what its strengths and weaknesses are. You'll also learn how to enable encryption for the OpenStack APIs.

Chapter 5, *Securing the OpenStack Identification and Authentication System and Its Dashboard*, shows you how the identification, authentication, and authorization systems work, as well as how OpenStack can be configured to meet your needs from this point of view.

Chapter 6, *Securing OpenStack Storage*, explains how the different kinds of storage work from a security standpoint and the options you have to implement them in OpenStack. Also, you will see some configuration to make the storage more resilient to attacks.

Chapter 7, *Securing the Hypervisor*, lists all the hypervisors that can be used with OpenStack. You'll find a lot of insight on how to choose the right hypervisor for you and how to secure it.

What you need for this book

To follow the examples in this book, you'll need an installation of OpenStack. This can be as big as multiple hardware machines or as little as a single virtual machine. For the goals of this book, it does not matter.

As for the operating system on the host, I suggest using CentOS/RHEL 6 or 7, because this is the configuration that is directly touched by the examples, but you can easily adapt the examples to any other Linux distribution.

Who this book is for

If you are an OpenStack administrator or developer, or wish to build solutions to protect your OpenStack environment, then this book is for you. Experience of Linux administration and familiarity with different OpenStack components is assumed.

Conventions

In this book, you will find a number of styles of text that distinguish between different kinds of information. Here are some examples of these styles, and an explanation of their meaning.

Code words in text, database table names, folder names, filenames, file extensions, pathnames, dummy URLs, user input, and Twitter handles are shown as follows: "You can find this configuration in the /etc/nova/policy.json file."

A block of code is set as follows:

```
<VirtualHost <ip address>:80>
  ServerName <site FQDN>
  RedirectPermanent / https://<site FQDN>/
</VirtualHost>
```

When we wish to draw your attention to a particular part of a code block, the relevant lines or items are set in bold:

```
policy_module(keystonewsgi, 1.0.0)

require {
  type httpd_t;
  type keystone_var_lib_t;
}
```

Any command-line input or output is written as follows:

```
$ echo "password" | md5sum
286755fad04869ca523320acce0dc6a4  -
```

 Warnings or important notes appear in a box like this.

 Tips and tricks appear like this.

Reader feedback

Feedback from our readers is always welcome. Let us know what you think about this book—what you liked or may have disliked. Reader feedback is important for us to develop titles that you really get the most out of.

To send us general feedback, simply send an e-mail to feedback@packtpub.com, and mention the book title via the subject of your message.

If there is a topic that you have expertise in and you are interested in either writing or contributing to a book, see our author guide on www.packtpub.com/authors.

Customer support

Now that you are the proud owner of a Packt book, we have a number of things to help you to get the most from your purchase.

Downloading the example code

You can download the example code files for all Packt books you have purchased from your account at http://www.packtpub.com. If you purchased this book elsewhere, you can visit http://www.packtpub.com/support and register to have the files e-mailed directly to you.

Errata

Although we have taken every care to ensure the accuracy of our content, mistakes do happen. If you find a mistake in one of our books—maybe a mistake in the text or the code—we would be grateful if you would report this to us. By doing so, you can save other readers from frustration and help us improve subsequent versions of this book. If you find any errata, please report them by visiting http://www.packtpub.com/submit-errata, selecting your book, clicking on the **errata submission form** link, and entering the details of your errata. Once your errata are verified, your submission will be accepted and the errata will be uploaded on our website, or added to any list of existing errata, under the Errata section of that title. Any existing errata can be viewed by selecting your title from http://www.packtpub.com/support.

Piracy

Piracy of copyright material on the Internet is an ongoing problem across all media. At Packt, we take the protection of our copyright and licenses very seriously. If you come across any illegal copies of our works, in any form, on the Internet, please provide us with the location address or website name immediately so that we can pursue a remedy.

Please contact us at copyright@packtpub.com with a link to the suspected pirated material.

We appreciate your help in protecting our authors, and our ability to bring you valuable content.

Questions

You can contact us at questions@packtpub.com if you are having a problem with any aspect of the book, and we will do our best to address it.

1
First Things First – Creating a Safe Environment

We often hear about security, but very often we do not receive a clear definition of what this is, since it's taken for granted. Even if we know what security in general is, sometimes we can miss some pieces of what security means in that specific field. I, personally, like to use this definition of information security – preservation of confidentiality, integrity, and availability of information.

The ISO/IEC 27000:2009 affirms that "In addition, other properties, such as authenticity, accountability, nonrepudiation, and reliability can also be involved."

This highlights the fact that security is a very wide sector, including two very different realms:

- Data protection from unauthorized access (confidentiality)
- Data integrity and availability

Before we dive in the security realm, we need to look at some important concepts of security.

Access control

Access control is the selective restriction of access to some kind of resource (a folder, a file, and a device). There are different types of approaches to access control. The first one is **Discretionary Access Control (DAC)** in which every user can decide who can, with which permissions, read his/her files.

An example of this is the Unix permission system where, if you create a file, you can choose who will be able to read or change it.

In **Mandatory Access Control** (**MAC**), the administrator decides the security policies and all the files in the system will comply.

An example of this is a public archive (that is, tax archive), where even if you are the creator of a document, you are not allowed to choose who is able to read it. Only the archive owner will be able to make such decisions.

An evolution of DAC and MAC is **Role-based Access Control** (**RBAC**). In RBAC, the permissions are not granted per user, but according to role. This allows big organizations to assign permission to roles and roles to users, making it easier to create, modify, or delete users.

Examples of this type of access controllers are pretty common in day-to-day life. A typical use of RBAC in real life is the *authorized personnel only* area, where usually all people with certain characteristics (that is, be it an employee of a specific company or be it the work for a specific department) are allowed to enter.

An evolution of RB and MAC is **Multi Level Security** (**MLS**). In MLS systems, each user has a trust level and each item has a confidentiality level. The administrator is still the one who is in charge of creating the security policies, as in MAC systems, but the system will ensure that each user will only see the items that have a confidentiality level allowed to him based on some system configurations and the user trust level.

The CIA model

As we have seen in the ISO 27000 definition, there are three words that are very important when speaking of security, Confidentiality, Integrity, and Availability. Even though many other models have been proposed over the years, the CIA model is still the one that is most used. Let's see the various parts of it.

Confidentiality

Confidentiality is the first part of the CIA model and is usually the first thing that people consider when they think about security. Many models have been created to grant the confidentiality of information, but the most famous and used by far is the Bell-LaPadula model. Implementing this model means creating multiple levels in which the users are divided and allowing all users of the nth level to read all documents collocated at any level lower or equal to n and to write documents at any level higher or equal to n. This is often characterized by the phrase *no read up, no write down*.

A lot of security attacks try to break the confidentiality of the data, mainly because it is a very lucrative job. Today companies and governments are willing to pay thousands or even millions of dollars to get information about their competitor's future products or a rival nation's secrets.

One of the easiest ways to grant confidentiality is by using encryption. Encryption cannot solve all confidentiality problems, since we have to be sure that the keys to decrypt the data are not stored with the data; otherwise, the encryption is pointless. Encryption is not the solution to every problem, since encrypting a data set will decrease performances of any operation over it (read/write). Also, encryption brings a possible problem — if the encryption key is lost, this will lead to losing the access to the data set, so encryption can become a hazard to the availability of the data.

You can think of confidentiality as a chain. A chain is as strong as its weakest link. I believe this is one of the most important things to remember about confidentiality, because very often we do a lot of work and spend a lot of money hardening a specific part of the chain leaving other parts very weak, nullifying all our work and the money spent.

I once had a client who engineers and designs his products in a sector where the average expense for R&D of a single product is way beyond the million USD. When I met them, they were very concerned about the confidentiality of one of their not yet released products, since they believed that it involved several years of research and was more advanced than their competitor's projects. They knew that if one of their competitors could obtain that information, he would have been able to fill the gap in less than 6 months. The main focus of this company was the confidentiality of the data; therefore, we created a solution that was based on a single platform (hardware, software, and configurations) and with a limited replication to maximize its confidentiality, even reducing its availability. The data has been divided into four levels based on the importance, using for-the-sake-of-clarity names inspired by the US Department of Defense system, and for each level we assigned different kinds of requirements, additional to the authorization:

- **Public**: All the information at this level was public for all, including people inside the company and outsiders, such as reporters. This information was something the company wanted to be public about. No security clearance or requirements were required.

- **Confidential**: All information at this level was available to people working on the project. Mainly for manuals and generic documentation, such as user manuals, repairman manuals, and so on. People needed to be authorized by their manager.

- **Secret**: All information at this level was available only to selected people working on the project and divided into multiple categories to fine grain permissions. This was used mainly for low-risk economical evaluations and noncritical blueprints. People needed to be authorized directly by the project manager and to use two factor authentications.

- **Top access control**: The information at this level was available only to a handful of people working on the project and was divided into multiple categories to fine grain permissions. It was used for encryption keys and all critical blueprints and economical and legal evaluations. People needed to be authorized directly by the project manager to use three-factor authentications and to be in specific high-security parts of the building.

All the information was stored on a single cluster and encrypted backups that were made daily were shipped to three secure locations. As you can see, Top Secret data could not exit from the building if not heavily encrypted. This helped the company to keep their advantage over competitors.

Integrity

By integrity we mean maintaining and assuring the accuracy and the consistency of the data during its entire lifecycle. The **Biba integrity model** is the most known integrity module and works exactly in the opposite way of the Bell-LaPadula model. In fact, it is characterized by the phrase *no read down, no write up*.

There are some attacks that are structured to destroy integrity. There are two possible reasons why a hacker would be interested in doing this:

- A lot of data has legal value only if its integrity has been maintained for the entire life span of the data. An example of this is forensic evidence. So, an attacker could be interested in creating reasonable doubt on the integrity of the data to make it unusable.

- Sometimes an attacker would like to change a small element of data that will affect future decisions that are based on that bit of data. An example can be an attacker who wants to edit the value of some stocks, so an automatic trading program would think that selling at a very low price would be a good idea. As soon as the automatic trading program does this transaction, the company (or bank) owning it would have lost a huge amount of money and will be very hard to trace back to the attacker.

An example of integrity is the Internet DNS service, which is a very critical service and has a core composed of a few clusters that have to grant integrity and availability. Availability is really important here because otherwise the Internet would be down for many users. However, its integrity is much more important, because otherwise an attacker could change a DNS value for a big website or a bank and create a perfectly undetectable phishing attack, also known as **pharming**, at a global scale. Each one of these clusters are managed by a different company or an organization, with different hardware, different software, and different configurations. Availability has been implemented using multiple hardware, software, and configurations to avoid the possibility of a faulty or hackable aspect that can bring down the whole system. Confidentiality is not the focus of this system since the DNS service does not contain any sensible data (or, at least, it shouldn't). Integrity is granted by a pyramidal system in which the top DNS (root DNS) is trusted by all other DNSes. Also, lately, all DNS programs are supporting encryption and untrustworthiness of unknown DNS servers to prevent DNS cache poison attacks, which have now become more frequent.

Availability

Availability simply means at any given moment, a document that should be available, **has** to be available. This means that no matter what has happened to your server, the main server farm, the data has to be available.

You can think of availability as a wire rope. A wire rope holds as long as at least one wire holds, so we can say that a wire rope is as strong as its strongest wire. Naturally, the lesser wires still in place, the more load they will have to carry, so they will be more susceptible to failures.

There is a type of attack that tries to reduce or put out availability, the Denial of Service attack. This family of attacks, also known as **DoS** or **DDoS** (if it's Distributed), has become very popular thanks to some groups such as **Anonymous**, and could create huge losses if the target system creates profits for the company. Also, often, these attacks are combined with attacks to steal the confidential information, since DoS attacks create a huge amount of traffic and could easily be used as a diversion.

In February 2014, CloudFlare, a big content delivery network and distributed DNS company, was attacked by a massive 400Gb/s DDoS attack that caused a huge slow down in CloudFlare services. This was the single biggest DDoS attack in history (until the end of 2014, when this book is being written). Lately, huge DDoS attacks are becoming more frequent. In fact from 2013 to 2014, DDoS attacks over 20Gb/s are doubled.

An interesting case I would like to relay here is the Feedly DDoS attack, which happened between July 10, 2014 and July 14, 2014. During this attack, Feedly servers had been attacked and a person, claiming to be the attacker, asked the company to pay some money to end the attack, which the Feedly company affirms not to have paid. I think this case gives us a lot to think about. Many companies are now moving towards a complete rely on computers, so new forms of extortion could become popular and you should start to think on how to defend yourself and your company.

Another type of DoS attack that is becoming more popular with the coming of public clouds, where you can virtually scale up your infrastructure unlimitedly is the **Economic Denial of Sustainability (EDoS)**. In this kind of attack, the goal is not to max out the resources since that would be pretty difficult, but it is to make it economically unsustainable for the company under attack. This kind of attack could even be a persistent attack where the attacker increases a company cloud bill of 10-20 percent without creating any income for the company. In the long run, this could make a company fail.

Some considerations

As you can imagine, based on the CIA model, there is no way a system can meet 100 percent of the requirements, because confidentiality, availability, and integrity are in contradiction. For instance, to decrease the probability of a leak (also known as loss of confidentiality), we can decide to use a single platform (hardware, software, and configuration) to be able to spend 100 percent of our efforts towards the hardening of this single platform. However, to grant better availability we should try to create many different platforms, as different as possible, to be sure that at least one would survive the attack or failure. How can we handle this? We simply have to understand our system needs and design the perfect mix of the two. I will go over a real-life example here that will give you a better understanding of mixing and matching your resources to your needs.

A real-world example

Recently, I helped a client to figure out how to store files safely. The company was an international company owning more than 10 different buildings in as many countries. The company has had few unhappy situations that lead it to consider it to be more important to keep the data safe. Specifically, the following things happened in the previous months:

- Many employees wanted to have an easy way to share their documents between their devices and with colleagues, so they often used unauthorized third-party services

- Some employees had been stopped at security controls in airports and the airport security had copied their entire hard drive
- Some employees had lost their phones, tablets, and computers full of company information
- Some employees had reported data loss after their computer hard drive failed and the IT team had to replace it
- An employee left the company revealing his passwords, locking the company out of his data

As often happens, companies decide to change their current system when multiple problems occurs, and they prefer to change to a solution that solves their problems altogether.

The solution we came up with was to create a multiregional cluster with Ceph, which provided the object storage we needed to put all the employer's data into. This allowed us to have multizone redundancy, which was necessary to grant availability. It also allowed us to create all backups in only two places instead of forcing us to have backups at all places. This increased the availability of backups and decreased their cost.

Also, client applications for computers, tablets, and phones have been created to allow the user to manage its files and automatically synchronize all files in the system. A nice feature of these clients is that they encrypt all the data with a password that is dynamically generated for each file and stored on another system (in a different data center) encrypted with the user **GNU Privacy Guard** (**GPG**) key. The user GPG key is also kept on an Hardware Security Module in a different Data Center to grant the company the possibility to decrypt a user's data if they leave. This granted a very high level of security and allowed to share a document between two or more colleagues.

The GPG key is also used to sign each file to grant that the file integrity has not been compromised.

To grant better security towards the loss or copy of computers, all company's computers have the hard drive completely encrypted with a key known only to the employer.

This solved all technical problems. To be sure that the people were trained enough to keep the system safe, the company decided to give a 5 days security course to all their employers and to add 1 day every year of mandatory security update course.

No further accidents happened in the company.

The principles of security

There are some principles that we always have to remember when we speak about IT security, since they can really help to prevent the most common security problems.

The Principle of Insecurity

I have called this principle the **Principle of Insecurity** because I have not yet found a better name for it. This principle states that no matter what you do, who you are, and how much money you spend, you will never have a 100 percent secure environment.

An example of this happened on April 7, 2014, when a new version of OpenSSL was published with the announcement of the Heartbleed bug having been fixed. This bug allowed users to extract a memory (RAM) dump from any machines that were running unpatched versions of OpenSSL. OpenSSL was considered safe and therefore the majority of the companies worldwide have used it and embedded it in their products to the point that in April 2014 there was close to no alternative to it. But even if something is very standard and wide used, it does not mean it's 100 percent secure.

Something that is always important to remember when we speak about security, is that money is limited, and it is often hard to evaluate how much money we can spend on security. To evaluate how much money it makes sense to spend on security, a mathematical economic model called the Gordon-Loeb model was developed in 2002, which tells us that it makes sense to spend up to 37 percent of the expected losses that would occur from a security breach. This model is widely used and is a well-accepted analytical model in the economics of cyber/information security literature.

> *Security is a journey, not a destination. Security is always an ongoing process.*

The Principle of Least Privilege

The **Principle of Least Privilege** (also known as the **Principle of Minimal Privilege** or the **Principle of Least Authority**) requires that any user, process, or system has all but only the permissions required to complete the assigned tasks. This is one of the most important principles on security and usually the one that is least considered.

I can write about many examples I have seen where the violation of this principle brought about very bad situations. Not very long ago, I saw a simple process that only needed to access (in read/write) one folder and to read from a database, wiping a machine and the multiple remote disks that were mounted in that moment, because the process was running as root instead of a limited user, as it should have.

What happened was that the process was removing all the files in a subdirectory with the bash command:

```
rm -rf $VAR/*
```

Here, the $VAR variable was set reading a field in the database. The database did not respond (because it was down) and therefore the variable was empty, allowing the process to run the following:

```
rm -rf /*
```

This is deadly if it is executed by root, since it will erase all the mounted storage devices, including the one containing the Operative System (the logs, etc.)

 When it comes to the Principle of Least Privilege, remember that rank does not mean full access. A company's CEO may need to see more data than other individuals, but he/she does not automatically need full access to the system just because he/she is the CEO.

The Principle of Separation of Duties

The **Principle of Separation of Duties** (also known as **Principle of Segregation of Duties**) requires that a complete task cannot be done by a person alone or that a person cannot perform all actions on a system. The basic idea of this principle is that completely trusting people could be unsafe for these reasons:

- People can make mistakes
- People can be malicious
- People can be corrupted or threatened
- People can take advantage of their position

This is always hard to accept for companies, but we have to face the fact that people are not perfect if we want to create a secure environment. The separation of duties (and powers, due to the Principle of Least Privilege) helps the people too, since they will be less prone to take advantage of their position and also they will be less attractive to those who wanted to bribe or threaten them.

A world-famous example of the consequences of failing to keep up with this principle is what happened at the **National Security Agency** (**NSA**) in 2013. On June 10, 2013 Edward Joseph Snowden, a private contractor working at NSA, leaked thousands of classified files from the NSA. This was possible because he was allowed to copy (and bring out of the facility) that data without the involvement of other people in the process.

People are often the weaker link of the security chain, so never underestimate people when thinking about security.

The Principle of Internal Security

The **Principle of Internal Security** requires that a system is defended by multiple layers of security, each one protecting it from a particular type of attack. Often this principle is stated not as a principle but as a technique with the name **Defense in depth** and **Castle Approach**. Data center designers should study a castle's fortification structure, since castles are very good examples of this principle. Very often, I see data centers with only one level of security and once you are able to violate it, you are free to go wherever you want. Castles, on the other hand, have multiple layers of security and even when you pass a security layer, you are still being watched. Also, the defenders in the towers will have a better spot than you because they are in enhanced security facilities, and there are no blind spots where you can hide.

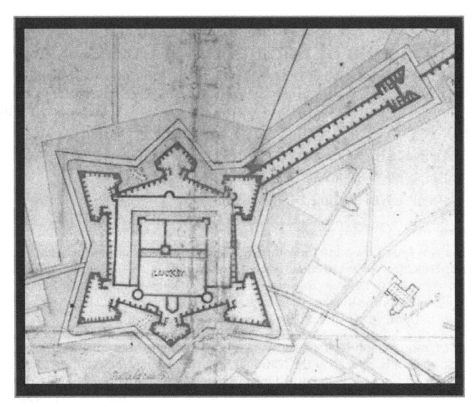

We have to design data centers with the idea that the single security layers (and potentially all security layers) could be breached. This means:

- Putting in multiple (different) security layers
- Monitoring in and around the security area, leaving no blind spot
- Training your people to react immediately to breaches
- Don't create strict reaction schemas, because if leaked, these could be used against you
- If breaches occur, study them and study countermeasures
- Run frequent tests to be sure all systems are active and your people are ready to react

IT security is as much about limiting the damage from breaches as it is about preventing them.

Data center security

Let's start with some things to remember when we design or verify the compliance of a data center. Very often, data centers are reused over the years for different kinds of data, so it's critically important to check every time that the data center is able to deliver enough security for the kind of data we are putting into it. Also, if we are designing a brand new data center, it would make sense to create it more secure than would suit the current needs (if it makes sense to spend the budget this way), so in the future it will be able to house more data without major work.

Many things that are very cheap or come free when you build something could become very expensive to fix later.

Select a good place

When I have to give my opinion on the location of a data center, I always try to consider any possible disaster that could happen in that location. For this reason, I strongly suggest to never build a data center on areas with high risk of earthquakes, floods, tornadoes, avalanches, or any other natural disaster you can think of. Also, I would suggest avoiding places where accidents can happen, such as places close to airports, highways, dangerous curved roads, power plants, oil refineries, chemical facilities, ammunition factories, and so on. These things are very important for the availability aspect of the CIA model, since those events could destroy your data center and will cause huge economical losses for the company as well as huge data loss. Also, those kind of places are often more expensive to protect with insurance, since they are more dangerous.

Implement a castle-like structure

As we have already seen, there are many similarities between castles and data centers, so we can learn a lot from history to harden our data centers.

First of all, we need a fence (or wall); this will be our first line of defense. This fence has to have one or two entry points (having more would cost much more and would not be very useful). Each of these entry points have to be guarded and have some hard security measures, such as retractable crash barriers. A bomb detector system could be put in place at any entrance if it is a possible risk.

The second line of defense should be a buffer zone between your facility and the fence. This area could be small (10 meters) or very big (100 meters) based on the facility needing security, the country you are building in, and your budget. This buffer zone has to be completely free, should offer no blind spot, and should be under complete surveillance. This will allow security to spot any attempt to bypass our fence. In case of fire, it will also prevent the fire from moving from your facility, to outside and from outside, to your facility and can be used as an assembly point. A parking space can be housed in this area, if it's distant enough from the building and placed in a way that does not confuse the security personnel.

The third line of defense will be the walls of our building. I usually consider the area delimited by this line of defense as the **secure zone**. Thick concrete walls are cheap and effective barriers against explosive devices and the elements. There are other materials that grant you a better level of security, but can be far more costly. This wall should have the least amount of openings. One or two accesses will be enough. Those accesses have to be guarded, and need surveillance cameras. Windows are not needed, and are usually dangerous. Fire doors have to be exit only, so install doors that do not have handles on the outside. Also, when any of these doors are opened, a loud alarm should sound and trigger a response from the security command center.

A fourth line of defense should be in place inside the building. This area will be designated as high security zone. This allows a third level of authorization, reducing the possibilities of unauthorized access. In this area, no food or liquids should be allowed.

A fifth line of defense could be in place, with another authorization point segmenting the server floor in multiple areas, where only people that have reasons to be in that particular area should be allowed to enter (for Principle of Least Privilege).

Secure your authorization points

As you can see, a lot of authorization points have to be put in place. How can we make an authorization point secure? By deploying man traps, we can use multifactor authentication. These measures can be used in one or more authorization points. Remember that all authorization points should be filmed and all accesses should be logged (in and out) for the record and make sure to check whether everyone left the building in case of an emergency or if there are people still trapped inside it.

Defend your employees

Even if a data center is more about computers than humans, people will have to be present in the data center for server maintenance, maintenance of the building, and security reasons. Make sure their life and health is always safe by providing safe places for them to stay and which give them a sense of security. Another thing that could be useful is a system that allows you to recirculate air rather than drawing in air from the outside. This could help protect people and equipment if there was some kind of biological or chemical attack or heavy smoke spreading from a nearby fire. For added security, it is possible to put devices in place to monitor the air for chemical, biological, or radiological contaminants.

Defend all your support systems

A data center has multiple support systems that have to be secured properly, such as power systems, air conditioner, etc. These systems should stay inside the secure zone or could have their own secure zone (another building within the buffer zone). Always remember that some of these systems can be dangerous themselves, so there has to be protection between them and the servers.

Keep a low profile

My father always says, "never let the thieves think you have something to steal"; this is a suggestion I always give my clients. If you start telling people that at this location you have a data center (or if you even paint on walls, like "[Company XYZ] Data Center"), don't be surprised if some thief comes to take a look.

Consider that you may put unworthy completely encrypted data in the data center, but the thieves will not know what data there is until they steal and analyze one or more disks. Furthermore, they might be interested in the servers themselves—even if bringing out hundreds of racks is not easy, they might be worth millions of dollars on the market.

Have you noticed how much attention the big companies (such as Amazon, Facebook, and Google) put on this? They do not allow people in their data centers unless they are invited. Some of these data centers have been filmed to create documentaries, but even those documentaries do not provide enough information on the data center's location and its security measures, so as to be sure that no one is too attracted by their data centers. Also, very often, the people who are not directly involved in the data center, will not know its exact position.

A hedge or some trees (outside the first fence zone) could help prevent curious people snooping on your site. Also, this prevents people seeing our security measures, this will decrease the probability of being the subject of casual attacks.

> *"Never let thieves think you have something to steal."*

The power of redundancy

When it comes to availability, there are two ways to provide it:

- Use high-end hardware that is failure proof
- Use redundancy

The high-end hardware is usually very expensive, includes redundancy, and is not as failure proof as it's usually sold as. Today, companies usually prefer redundancy of common hardware because it is cheaper, is able to grant better availability, and is easier to deploy and maintain.

When I was starting in the IT field, it was not really clear to me which degree of redundancy was right and which was not. Luckily for me, after a few months of field work, I have had a very interesting conversation about this with a senior technician which explained to me very clearly:

> *"A system has enough redundancy if I can unplug and replug all cables, one cable at a time, and no user complains."*

Cameras

I have already said this about some specific areas, but it's true for all areas. There should be no blind spot in the camera system and each camera should be in the visual field of at least one other camera.

Also, the recording should be kept in case of a break in, in order to be analyzed to prevent the success of future attempts using the same method.

Blueprints

The legend goes that the pharaohs of Egypt killed the pyramid architects to be sure that the blueprint remained a secret. No matter whether this is true or not, the concept that this legend underlines is surely true: the pharaohs did not want the blueprints of their pyramid in the hands of the thieves.

The same thing should be done by companies too. Inviting visitors to see the high level of security can be counterproductive because an observant visitor could spot some security flaws. Also, this removes the surprise aspect. In fact, if the attacker passed the second layer of security and has no idea about how many other levels there could be, he might be less willing to go forward. Furthermore, it could happen that you are able to open the first door of a man-trap (That is because he stole a badge) but you could fail the biometrical authentication needed to open the second door because you were not expecting it, resulting in a locked man-trap with no possibility to exit.

Data center in office

Often, people ask me what I think about dedicating a room in the office as a data-center. I believe this kind of approach is less safe even if it is well implemented, and very often it is also implemented poorly from a security stand point. I can understand that sometimes the need for security is way less than the one provided by a dedicated facility (always remember the Gordon-Loeb model). In these cases, I strongly suggest to implement it as best as possible and to extend some security policies for the whole building.

Often, I have seen data centers in offices implemented as racks in the CTO office, or even as racks in the lobby. Do not do this, as they will make any other efforts to secure your environment useless and a huge waste of resources.

An example of a good implementation of a data center in an office will be:

- An hedge to protect the propriety
- A fence (with guarded entrance)
- The parking lot
- A 10 meters buffer zone
- A building (with guarded entrance)
- A secure zone that can be accessed by employees and escorted visitors (with man-trap access)

- A secure elevator requiring an authorized badge to go to the data center floor (this will be the high security zone)
- A man-trap entrance to the data center with multifactor authentication
- Eventual doors in the data center for granular access

This way you are able to keep multiple authorization points without having to use a different facility. This is still less secure than a dedicated facility, but can be a good balance between security and cost. Also, this will make the whole office more secure.

Server security

At this point, we have covered some basic rules and tips on how to implement a safe data center. Let's move to the next step: the security inside the data center.

As we have already mentioned in the preceding paragraphs, we can split the servers with secure doors for more granular access. Why should we do this? Isn't it enough to be sure that all people entering the data center are authorized? Very often this is not enough because all the people who are authorized to enter in the data center will be allowed to touch every single device in it so we are still not compliant with the Principle of Least Privilege.

Some companies solve this problem with a locked rack, while others resolve it with segmented data centers, or even with both approaches. Both the approaches have ups and downs, for instance, you might prefer a segmented data center approach because:

- Rack doors are often uncomfortable and require a wider aisle
- Open racks have a better air flow than locked racks (this is not always true)
- Open racks are way cheaper than locked racks

This approach also has some disadvantages:

- Less flexible (the person has or has not access to multiple racks)
- Walls and doors have to be placed during the data center construction and cannot be moved later

A combined solution can solve some of these disadvantages. Another mixed option is the locking cages, which are easier to install than walls but are often easier to break in.

To implement more, the Separation of Duties principle is possible to require two authorized people to be present at the same time to unlock a door or it could require a badge of type A for unlocking the doors in the data center and a badge of type B to unlock the racks.

This measure will increase security, but your administrators will be way less productive because there will always be two people doing the work of a single person. It could make sense on critical systems while not on all the other systems.

The importance of logs

Often my clients ask me what they should log and what they should not log. My usual answer is. "What would you like to know if an accident or a data leak would have just happened?" I think this is the whole point, you have to think in the various scenarios which kind of data you would like to have and then start collecting them immediately. The same answer is valid for "For how long should I keep this log?"

 The importance of logs is that those are the only traces that can help you to understand what exactly happened and why.

Where to store the logs?

There are many places where you can store the logs, such as:

- Files on filesystems
- Files on SAN or other replicated infrastructure
- Lines in a relational and or transactional database
- Lines in a NoSQL database

The first option seems very good because hard drives are pretty cheap and you only need a server with a lot of hard drives to make it work. The downsides of this option are multiple:

- **Unreliability**: How can you be sure whether the machine will be up today or tomorrow?
- **Scalability**: How will you handle the case in which all your drives will be full?
- **Read performances**: How much time will you need to scan all your logs? (consider that data center grade hard drive usually can read between 100MB/s and 200MB/s)
- **Usability**: How will you find the exact data you need?

The second option does solve the first two disadvantages of the first option, but still has the usability issue and can be very costly.

The third option does solve the usability problem, but based on the fact that you have one or more nodes, can show the unreliability and the read performances problems. No matter how you design the node or cluster, you will have huge scalability problems and also some constraints created by the rigid structure of tables.

The last option does solve all problems in my opinion. Even if technically speaking it is a very good option, it will bring some aspects to be considered:

- You will need someone with NoSQL/Big Data experience
- You will have a high initial cost because NoSQL databases usually need more than three nodes to create a cluster.

While speaking of OpenStack, the best option to store log is OpenStack Data Processing Service (Sahara), since it's a part of OpenStack since October 2014.

The more information you log and with more details, the harder is it to store them and retrieve them. In fact, if you only store one type of data (for example, the time and person that is logging in a machine), you will probably have a few megabytes of data every month and; therefore, it will be very easy to put it in a relational database (such as MariaDB or PostgreSQL) that you already have in place. This is also possible because we have only one kind of data; you can know exactly how each log entry will be presented to your log system. When you start logging thousands of lines per hour, coming from tens or hundreds of sources, and with tens of different formats, the NoSQL storage seems to be the only one that works.

Evaluate what to log

Although there is no ultimate solution for deciding what logs work for every company, since every company is different, there are some things that are usually logged:

- Door access (both entering and exiting)
- Server access (SSH, Database, and so on)
- All servers logs
- Data center environmental metrics (temperature, humidity, and so on)

It's really important that a considered decision is made here to ensure that you have all the logs you need, but on the other hand you will not save a huge amount of logs that you will never use.

Evaluate the number of logs

Another important thing to decide is for how long to keep the logs. Some countries have specific laws for the minimum time to keep some kinds of logs, while other do not. In my opinion, it depends a lot from company to company, but I usually suggest keeping them for at least 1 year.

A whole year seems to be a lot of time, but it's not; it's the very minimum in my opinion. This is because if you suspect that a person lately is behaving strangely, you will want to look the logs for at least one year to confirm a pattern or a change of pattern.

The best option of all is to keep logs indefinitely, so that you can really go back in the past and have full information about the past.

The people aspect of security

I have seen, in my life, many more security problems caused by humans than machines. With the people aspect of security I mean all human actions that can increase or decrease security. Humans are in the vast majority of company processes, and can often be the weak link of the chain in multiple occasions, such as in the following examples:

- A system administrator disables a firewall (or allows all by default) to speed up a process
- A system administrator sends a PEM certificate/PGP private key by e-mail
- A user creates a weak password to remember it better
- A user writes his password on a piece of paper stitched to the monitor
- A user gives his password to a colleague via his phone

As you can see, there are some actions that are committed by system administrators, while others are committed by users, but at the end of the day, they can have a huge impact no matter who committed it. Some of these actions can be prevented using automatic systems, such as using a password grader before accepting a password. Some other actions can be prevented only informing your users and system administrators and teaching them to act properly for your company security and their own.

I divide the human aspect of security in the following categories:

- Simple forgetfulness
- Shortcuts
- Human error
- Lack of information
- Social engineering
- Malicious actions under threats
- Malicious actions for own advantage

Simple forgetfulness

This is a very common pattern in humans. Very often, people perform actions without really caring or not thinking about the consequences of their actions. The most commons cases in this category are:

- A user creates a weak password to remember it better
- A user writes his password on a piece of paper stitched to the monitor
- A user gives his password to a colleague via his phone

As you can see, I have listed only user actions, because very often those errors are committed by users, not system administrators. The good news for you is that these kinds of errors are usually easy to spot, fix, and prevent.

I have worked in a company that needed to increase its security, so we started working on this because is very cost effective. We started assessing the passwords using John the Ripper in a secure machine on the hashed passwords. The result was shocking—more than 95 percent of the passwords were found in less than an hour on an average computer. We decided to create a very small course (2 hours) in which we explained how to create safe passwords and how to handle them safely. The course has been forced to all employees in the following week. After the week ended, we created a JavaScript, was been loaded on any login page, which checked whether the password in its current form was secure enough, and if not, changed the reference URL of the login button so that the first page proposed to the user was the change password page. After one week, we ran the John the Ripper test again and with much joy we have seen that the first password has been found after more than 24 hours in the test and in 24 hours we were still under the 1 percent of passwords found. The policies we enforced were the following:

- No dictionary word

- At least one uppercase letter, one lowercase letter, one number and a special character, excluding '!', '#', '@', '&', and '$' which are the most common special characters

- At least thirteen character-long passwords

Using these three rules, we removed the weak passwords problem, reaching 80 bits of entropy on each password.

 The **National Institute of Standards and Technology (NIST)** suggested to use at least 80 bits of entropy for secure passwords.

To be sure that the people followed the instructions given during the password course to manage the passwords, we identified a few people in the company who were most successful during the course, to help out with looking for colleagues that were handling the passwords unsafely. Those people caught handling unsafe passwords were signed up for another course (4 hours, this time), which was more focused on giving the reasons as to why people should follow the rules, rather than simply teaching them the rules (that were already discussed in the previous course).

As for password sharing and other similar practices, a system has been put in place to be sure that no more than an IP could use a certain username and password at a given moment in time. If more than a user did connect, the account was locked automatically and the user (owner of the account) had to call the IT department directly to ask them to unlock his account. In a few months, these kind of actions will no longer happen. We did not solve the password over telephone problem directly (because is not possible to enforce this kind of rule, unless there is someone listening for all phone calls, which is pretty impossible), but we have made it pretty noticeable by the IT department.

Shortcuts

People are lazy and will try to use any possible shortcut that they can think of. I know this is a huge generalization, but it's true more often than not. If you ask people to do a complex process and they see the possibility of having similar results with a much simpler process, the majority of them will use the simpler process and this is more true, when the same person has to do the same process multiple times.

How can you defend your company from this? The first thing to do is to keep the processes as simple as possible, so that people have less advantages to take a shortcut. The second thing to do is to inform all the people that are part of each process the reasons why that process is done in that way and what can be the consequences of a different process.

To explain this at best, I'd like to bring you a very famous example from a different field, aviation. British Airways Flight 5390 became famous because on June 10, 1990, since an windscreen blew due to a panel that was improperly installed. In the process, the captain of the plain, Tim Lancaster, was ejected halfway out of the aircraft. The body of the captain (still alive) was firmly pressed against the window frame where it stayed until the first officer managed to perform an emergency landing in Southampton with no loss of life.

The reason this accident is of such importance is that it shows what can happen when enough information about a process is given to the people who are executing that process. In this case, the problem was that in a replacement done few hours before the flight, the windscreen had been changed and wrong bolts were used. In fact, 84 of the 90 windscreen retention bolts were 0.026 inches (0.66 mm), which is too short in diameter, while the remaining six were 0.1 inches (2.5 mm), too short. This has been possible because the operator that changed the windscreen used a **like for like** method to select the new bolts, instead of looking up on the maintenance documentation, even if this would have been the right procedure following the official British Airways policies, which required referencing to the maintenance documentation for each component that is being replaced on the planes.

Three out of the five recommendations of the Civil Aviation Authority following this accident, aimed to improve the probability of the right execution of the procedures by the people, mainly through training, and testing including the possible consequences of shortcuts during the processes. The remaining two recommendations were about examining the continued viability of self-certification with regards to safety critical tasks on aircraft and about recognizing the need for the use of corrective glasses, if prescribed, in association with aircraft engineering tasks.

Human error

Human errors are very frequent and usually have disastrous consequences. One of the main causes of human errors in IT, in my experience, is pressure.

Human error implies that the person doing the action knows what he/she should do, but does it differently because there are external factors acting on them, such as pressure or tiredness.

I have not seen a single office in my life that was not susceptible to pressure or tiredness—obviously a good management can help, but cannot prevent it. What you can do is document everything when you are calm and rested, so when pressure or tiredness grow, it is possible to follow the documentation.

I have seen this in multiple companies' IT departments with no documentation. I know this is pretty common (at least in south Europe) because multiple colleagues of mine have told me that they have had similar experiences. I do remember a specific case in which I went to a company to create an active-active cluster.

 In my experience, the presence of documentation for certain procedures creates less pressure on the executors; therefore, the simple fact of having a procedure can decrease one of the cause of errors.

After a few days in the job, the main MySQL database went down and the manager asked me to fix it. After a little bit of analysis, I had in place a workaround promoting the slave to the master, so that the company was able to work again. This was obviously a dirty workaround that had to be fixed very soon. So, after working for hours, when it was safe to shut down the system for enough time, we created a new slave to restore the initial situation. I have asked the manager if this ever happened before and how they fixed it the previous times. He responded saying that it already happened few times, but the person who fixed it the previous time left the company months ago leaving no documentation, since the company never forced him to write it. Having all data on a SAN, we chose to do a SAN copy to improve the speed of the recovery. The result has been a huge mess with doubled LVM IDs that required more than 2 hours to be cleared.

Obviously, I cannot blame the previous technician for the LVM issue, but if he/she would have written a documentation for that procedure, we would have followed it without creating the mess, considering that all that mess happened because a single LVM command had been forgotten planning the work.

Lack of information

As we have seen, human errors and shortcuts are often caused by a lack of information. Sometimes, the lack of information does not result in human errors or shortcuts, but ends up in disasters because the person that is doing the procedure does not know something relevant to the procedure, or has no real idea about the environment it is working on.

The solution is to create the documentation and to update it constantly. Obviously, it is important to read all the documentation too. In my experience, it is really important to have a good tool for documentation. Some companies use Word documents or similar kind of programs. I think this is wrong for mainly the following four reasons:

- Word processors mix style with the content, which can create problems when you have commands and code in your documentation
- It's not possible, or very hard, to link each document or section. Every time a system or procedure is mentioned, it will be linked. Each system should have a page with all procedures and configuration linked, and vice versa.
- It requires specific software or other kind of not-so-friendly interfaces (such as Google Drive)
- It does not support (or supports small) versioning

I think the best way to provide documentation is with a wiki installation or a Git repository containing human readable documentation in a markdown or a similar format. If you go for the Git repository option, remember to export them in HTML too, to be more accessible. In either case, remember to backup your documentation frequently because it's a very important asset.

 Always create a documentation of everything you do, because later on you or someone else will need it.

Social engineering

"The information security industry defines social engineering as an attack that breaches an organization's security defenses by manipulating people and the human tendency to trust." – SysAdmin Audit Networking and Security Institute (SANS Institute)

Humans are in pretty much all processes or can enter into them if they feel the urgency to do so. Humans, also, are very often the weakest link of a security chain since they are flexible, while computers are not.

 Humans are flexible and usually try to meet other people's expectations, often accepting a rule violation to do so.

Today, it's possible to create a secure system for a small amount of money that will require multiple times more money to break into it. This is the reason why attackers use people inside the company to drastically reduce the amount of effort needed to break into the system. The majority of times, the attacker exploits the employee's willingness to meet the other person's expectation to get the information they need.

Lately, social engineering has been split into tens of fields based on the vehicle of attack and the goal. We will not go deeper in this topic at the moment.

I would like to bring you an example of social engineering I did, because I didn't believe what happened would have been so easy in that company.

I was placed in a big company to help them increase their security. The manager was willing to undertake a lot of actions in this sense, but thought that social engineering was only a commercial thing used by sellers to sell more useless services and therefore was not willing to implement any social engineering countermeasure. To demonstrate to him the importance of social engineering countermeasures, I pulled out my phone, and called the company front desk hiding my number. I informed the person who responded that I had problems with an invoice calculation, and therefore had to speak with someone in the accounting department. Soon after a person of the accounting department responded. I informed him that I was calling from Microsoft helpdesk and that I had to do some tests with him due to a new update that has been rolled out that morning. The man was really happy about my call because he also had a problem with a scanner that was not able to make it work properly. I said that a part of the procedure required his company password and a lot of other data to verify that everything worked. The incredible part was that he gave me all the information without doubting my intentions. While I was on the phone, the manager was shocked that an employee had shared so much information with an unknown person over the phone.

Evil actions under threats

Sometimes the attacker is not able to circumvent anyone in the company, so he/she might want to identify a person who has enough clearance and is easy to threaten to obtain what we are looking for. In movies, usually, the villain kidnaps a person from the hero's family to obtain what he is looking for. Luckily, in reality, this is not common and usually the threats are much smaller, but still work for the attacker's purpose.

My point of view is that it is really important that the company works to ensure their employees work in a secure environment mainly limiting their powers. Mistreating someone is very dangerous and legally speaking very bad in the majority of countries; therefore, the attacker would like to get a single person with enough power, but if there are no people with this power, an attacker could try different approaches to the problem leaving aside the employees.

Evil actions for personal advantage

I have left this category as the last one because it's often hard to accept, mainly in small companies, and very hard to deal with.

Sometimes people commit evil actions and you have to be prepared for this. This kind of inside attack is usually very dangerous because they will be able to ask for favors from their colleagues with legitimacy. If they do not have direct access to the resource they need, they can use social engineering but using their real credentials to gain more trust and to be able to ask for bigger favors or more confidential information.

For this reason, you have to segment the process and have very strict rules that don't allow a person to know more than they are meant to know. Also, it is important to inform your employees and make them aware of this kind of risk.

Summary

In this chapter, we have seen an introduction to security as well as a number of best practices to use. These best practices will help you to have a safer environment.

Often, people focus so strongly on securing a system from a specific kind of attack that the system seems inexpugnable from that point of view, but they forget to secure the system from other prospective too, making worthless or their work.

In the next chapter, we will dive into some security challenges you may be facing and into the OpenStack structure.

2
OpenStack Security Challenges

As we have seen in the first chapter, each level of your infrastructure can be an object of the unwanted attention for an attacker. Software is no exception to this. There are a lot of attacks that aim to find bugs or misconfigurations in software and exploit them to gain access to the machines that run the software, or to data. OpenStack, with all its parts and all the software it relies on, can be a very effective attack vehicle if not safely configured, due to its very trustful policy that allows nodes to access all data if the node requires it. So, an attacker can quickly compromise and obtain your data if he or she is able to compromise a single node.

Before looking at OpenStack directly, I would like to deal with a critical aspect: security in cloud environments; that is, the ownership of machines.

In this chapter, we will to cover:

- The differences between the private and the public cloud with a focus on the security aspects
- The possible security threats to a cloud components of OpenStack

Private cloud versus public cloud security

Very often people say **cloud** when they actually mean **public cloud**. For this reason, in the book, we'll always specify **private cloud** or **public cloud** and when we do not specify anything, the word cloud is used in both senses at the same time.

This is a necessary disclaimer because when speaking of security, private and public clouds have completely different issues, but let's start from the beginning.

The private cloud

A private cloud environment is operated solely for a single organization (or person) by internal or third-party personnel. In a private cloud situation, all machines are owned (or leased) by the organization and will run that organization's software exclusively.

From an economical perspective, private clouds are less flexible; in fact, the number of machines will stay pretty stable over time compared to public clouds.

From a scalability perspective, private clouds are not very flexible because you can't use more processing power than that you have installed it with. Very often, private clouds are kept with an average of 80-90 percent load and this means you can burst only 10-25 percent of your average load.

From a security perspective, private clouds grant you full access (and full responsibilities) to create a safe environment. This means that no one can look at your data if you create a safe environment, and you will have to spend money to create a safe environment. Usually, these clouds are created behind a company's firewall, so this helps secure them. This security advantage is negated if the cloud contains the Web-readable/writable content because you'll have to open your firewall ports in this case. This is often mitigated by creating two different clouds, one for web-accessible data (in a DMZ) and one that is accessible only by internal users (in the internal network).

The public cloud

> *"There is no [public] cloud, only other people's computers."* – *Free Software Foundation Europe*

A public cloud has very different problems and opportunities as compared to a private cloud.

From an economical perspective, with a public cloud, you pay exactly what you use as you go, so no upfront costs.

From a scalability perspective, public clouds can be considered as limitless because they usually have so many resources available that you can start up all the machines you need without worrying about cloud capabilities.

From a security perspective, the public cloud is more complex to analyze. Since cloud providers usually provide to millions of machines at any given moment, they can invest way more than the average company for security. Thus, their cloud is very secure. The drawback is that you have to trust the **Cloud Service Provider (CSP)** completely with your data. If the CSP would like to see your data and everything you run on their machines, they can. If they are interested in selling your data to your competitor, there are very limited things you can do. Also, we have to remember that public clouds can be attacked from inside, since an attacker can lease a virtual machine directly into the cloud for a few dollars and without any questions asked.

 Since all users of a public cloud are not in the company network of the cloud service provider, public clouds have to be accessible from the Web, increasing the attack surface of public clouds.

Private cloud versus public cloud

The following is an easy-to-remember schema that will help you immediately understand the advantages and disadvantages of public and private clouds:

Prospective	Public cloud	Private cloud
Economical	Pay as you go	Pay upfront
Bandwidth	Usually very high	Limited
Scalability	Virtually unlimited	Limited
Security	Usually very high	Limited to your budget
Data confidentiality	Not under your control	Under your control
People you have to trust	Yourself and the cloud provider	Yourself

As we can see, public clouds and private clouds are very different and there isn't a choice that is always right and one that is always wrong. It depends on the specific software you have to deploy. If you integrate a private cloud with a public cloud, you'll have an **hybrid cloud**. Usually, the public part of a hybrid cloud has the same characteristics as that of a public cloud, as the private part has the same characteristics of a private cloud.

The different kinds of security threats

As we have seen in the previous chapter, when we speak about security, we can mean multiple things. Also, as we have just seen that private and public clouds present different kinds of security issues. We are now going to analyze the various attacks that you can encounter when administering an OpenStack cloud.

Possible attackers

Let's start by identifying the possible attackers we can face. They can be divided in different ways based on their goals; in this case, we will distinguish them as the following:

- **Automated attacks/Script kiddies**: Automated vulnerability scanning/ exploitation.

- **Motivated individuals**: This includes multiple kinds of attackers, such as small-scale industrial espionage, rogue or malicious employees, or disaffected customers. They act alone.

- **Highly capable groups**: These groups often refer to themselves as **Hacktivist** and are not typically commercially funded, but can pose a serious threat to service providers and cloud operators. Many groups of hackers have organized themselves lately, such as Lulzsec and Anonymous.

- **Organized hackers**: These are groups of hackers who are usually highly capable. These groups are financially driven and able to fund in-house to exploit development and target research. Multiple groups fall in this category, from the Russian Business Network to the various organized groups that undertake industrial espionage.

- **Intelligence agencies/services**: They usually have capabilities greater than any other attacker, because they can bend rules without breaking them and can be authorized to violate rules. Intelligence agencies and other governmental players are comparable to organized hackers, but usually have far more money they can spend on those operations, making them more effective.

The possible attacks

There are multiple kinds of attacks that can be put into action. The main kinds are as follows:

- Denial of Service
- 0-day

- Brute force
- Advanced Persistent Threat
- Automated exploitation tools
- ISP intercept
- Supply chain attack
- Social engineering
- Hypervisor Breakout

Denial of Service

A **Denial of Service (DoS)** attack is an attack that aims to make some service unavailable. In the last few years, usually we speak about DDoS, since those are very effective and cheap and for those reasons have become the most used DoS attack. DDoS attacks consist in multiple machines trying to overload a server or its connection to make the services that are running on that server unavailable.

The good part about DoS attacks is that in majority of the cases, as soon as they end it, all is back to normal. When this is not true, small actions have to be executed by system administrators, such as restarting a service or rebooting a machine.

 There is no way to completely protect a server from a DoS attack.

Even if you cannot protect your company completely from such attacks, you can mitigate them in two ways:

- Having a lot of spare resources such as CPU, RAM, and bandwidth makes harder to knockdown the service
- Writing rules on firewalls (or having an **Intrusion Prevention System** (IPS) or an **DoS Defense System** (DDS) that do it for you) that drop all traffic coming from IPs that are currently attacking your servers

There are companies that provide **clean pipes** that are connected with only good traffic since have already been filtered by the ISP using IPSes and DDSes.

Usually, DDoSes are used by automated attacks/script kiddies, motivated individuals, and highly capable groups. It could so happen that organized hackers too use DDoS attacks, but, in this case, it's usually an **Advanced Persistent DoS** (**APDoS**), where the attack lasts for long periods (the longest APDoS registered was 38 days), moves from server to server to be harder to detect, and involves a huge amount of traffic (usually more than 50Pb in total).

In the history of DoS attacks, the following methods have been heavily used:

- **Buffer overflow attacks**: In this kind of attack, the attacker looks for buffers that are filled with input from the user without prior validation. Since buffers have a fixed length, we can't put only a certain amount of data that can fit in the buffer; the rest of the data will be written in other parts of RAM and could be executed by the program.

- **SYN Flood attacks**: As we will see more deeply in the next chapter, the computers expect certain handshakes at the beginning of a communication. This attack violates this convention forcing the server to open more connections than needed. At a certain point, the server will not be able to open a new connection, making the service unavailable.

- **Teardrop attacks**: Network packages should be of certain sizes. If bigger packages are found, the machines split them into smaller packages to manage them properly. Old machines have problems recognizing and properly managing packages that are smaller than expected. In this attack, this bug is exploited by sending smaller packages than expected to the machines, which in old systems often resulted in system crashes and reboots.

- **Smurf attacks**: In this kind of attack, the attacker uses badly configured machines in the network to amplify the attack. Usually, the attacker sends a forged package (that is, ICMP ECHO package) that seems to arrive from the victim to a broadcast address. All the machines in the broadcast domain that are tricked by this package, will respond to the victim. So, if in the network there are 100 machines with poor configuration, an attacker could be able to create an amount of traffic that is 100 times its maximum amount of traffic.

- **Viruses/Worms**: In this kind of attack, the attacker creates a self-replicating program that can consume resources or destroy the systems.

0-day

A 0-day attack is an attack that exploits a vulnerability that was not known (or thought not to be exploitable) until that day. In these cases, there is no patch available when the attack is used the first time.

In a 0-day case, no specific measurement can protect a company, but all general security measurements we already talked about in the previous chapter will help mitigate this risk.

0-day attacks can only be done by highly capable groups, organized hackers, and intelligence agencies/services because those are the only players that have the resources needed to do such an attack.

Brute force

Since many attackers cannot afford to invest to research 0-day attacks, they use Brute force. Brute force is very noisy and the majority of system administrators, and IDSes will recognize and block them.

To prevent these kinds of attacks, you should have an IDS and good policies for passwords.

These attacks are so noisy that only automated attacks/script kiddies and motivated individuals will use them.

Advanced Persistent Threat

An **Advanced Persistent Threat (APT)** is a kind of attack in which expert attackers use stealthy and continuous attacks targeting a specific entity.

During an APT attack, it is common to find many attacks that we already discussed, such as APDoS, and 0-day exploitations. Often also involved are Social Engineering techniques and Supply Chain attacks, which we will talk about shortly.

Since these are very expensive attacks that require multiple people, they can only be done by highly capable groups, organized hackers, and intelligence agencies/services.

Automated exploitation tools

Since APT attacks are very expensive, automated attacks/script kiddies, and motivated individuals will prefer **Automated exploitation tools**. These tools allow the attacker to test multiple already known exploits to search for a known exploit that the system administrator has not yet patched.

Examples of Automated exploitation tools are **Metasploit** and **Nessus**.

 To prevent these kinds of attacks, you need to always keep your system updated and frequently check online whether there are new ways to exploit software applications you use become known.

The ISP intercept

The ISP intercept is a category in which a lot of possible attack vectors fall into. The baseline is that somehow the attacker is able to see all traffic moving into your connection at the border of your property. This attack can be executed legally by Intelligence agencies/services with a warrant, or could be executed illegally.

I've seen an example of an illegal execution of this kind of attack in a company, where the attacker has cut the company's Internet connection cable and has added its own box that allowed the traffic to be normally received and sent, but also copied all the passing data to the attacker systems.

Preventing those kinds of attacks is impossible because they are executed outside your competence limits. The only possible way to mitigate these attacks is to encrypt all the data you share with the outside world.

Sometimes even companies' private networks can be compromised with this attack. Recently, there have been rumors that the NSA was able to retrieve data from Google and Yahoo! by tapping their fiber optics cables that connect the datacenters. Even if there hasn't been any official confirmation, in a few months' since these rumors, both Google and Yahoo! announced that they now encrypt all traffic between datacenters to prevent this from happening.

The only kind of attacker that can do this legally are the Intelligence agencies/ services. But organized hackers can also perpetrate such attacks.

The supply chain attack

In a supply chain attack, the attacker tempers a cryptographic component, such as a device that performs encryption or secure transactions, when it is still in the supply chain of the device, so that it is not yet in the hands of the client. This could happen during the manufacture of the device or at a certain point before it is put into the production environment. For this kind of attack, the attacker needs physical access to the device. A common type of tempering is the installation of a rootkit or specific hardware design to spy on the user.

From the documents written by *Edward Snowden*, it seems that the NSA has been able to perform multiple Supply Chain Attacks in the last few years. This has not been confirmed as of today by the NSA itself.

Due to its complexity, only Organized hackers and Intelligence agencies/services can perform this kind of attack.

Social engineering

As we have already seen in the previous chapter, social engineering could be a good option for an attacker who would like to attack an organization.

All kinds of attackers can perform social engineering attacks, but the most effective will be the ones perpetrated by the most skilled groups.

The Hypervisor breakout

Since we are focusing on OpenStack, the **Hypervisor breakout** is an attack your company could suffer from.

In an Hypervisor breakout, the user of a virtual machine is able to escape from his virtual machine and connect to the host that is running the virtual machine. In the history of virtualization, there have been multiple cases of possible Hypervisor Breakout attacks and pretty much all hypervisors have been objects of such unwanted attention.

At the moment, there is no known case of Hypervisor Breakout in real-world attacks, but it is possible that some companies have been compromised by this kind of feature but has not made it public due to the possible consequences to the company's image.

The real risk with an attack of this kind is that a person with such a level of access will probably be able to attack every machine in the cluster and will be able to access all resources available to those machines.

We will see how to prevent this kind of attack in the last chapter of this book.

These attacks are really hard to perform and are very expensive, so only organized hackers and intelligence agencies/services will be able to perform them.

The OpenStack structure

OpenStack is an orchestration suite to create clouds mainly focused to create **Infrastructure as a Service (IaaS)** solutions. OpenStack has multiple components, each one aiming to provide a piece to the cloud. As I write, last OpenStack stable version is Juno that has the following components:

OpenStack Compute Service – Nova

Computing is one of the core parts of any IaaS solution, as well as OpenStack. This is also one of the two oldest modules of OpenStack, since it has been part of the project since its first version, Austin, which was released in October, 2010. Nova derives from NASA's Nebula platform.

Nova is a cloud computing fabric controller. It is designed to manage and automate pools of computer resources and can work with many hypervisors such as KVM, VMware, and Xen.

It is written in Python and uses many external libraries. Nova was created with horizontal scalability in mind; in fact, it's able to scale horizontally on **commercial off-the-shelf** (COTS) components. This allows you to keep the hardware costs down and to easily integrate with legacy hardware.

Starting from the Havana release, Nova is able to run docker containers directly, but due to some Continuous-Integration problems, this feature will be in the main source code only since the Kilo release.

Nova can be compared to Amazon's **Amazon Elastic Compute Cloud (EC2)**. As for the Docker addition in Kilo, Amazon provides the **AWS Elastic Beanstalk** service.

OpenStack Object Storage Service – Swift

The other component available since the first release of OpenStack is Swift, a scalable redundant storage system. Swift was developed in the first place by Rackspace Hosting itself and derives from the Rackspace expertise, and is built for creating and managing the Rackspace Hosting Cloud File service. Currently, Swiftstack is leading the development of Swift.

Swift is an object storage capable to ensure data integrity, thanks to its ability to write the files to multiple disks spread throughout the nodes in the cluster. Swift is also able to manage multiple regions for the same pool, so it's possible to create real-time, off-site replicas of data to prevent possible data losses in case of problems in the main region.

Due to its design, Swift—like Nova—is created with horizontal scalability in mind, and works with COTS components.

Swift can be compared to Amazon's **Amazon Simple Storage Service (S3)**.

OpenStack Image Service – Glance

Glance has been added in the second release of OpenStack (Bexar), and since its first version, it has greatly improved. Glance is useful to save disk and server images to make the users able to run multiple equal servers without having to reconfigure them each time.

The purpose of Glance is to help you manage the Nova images in a simpler and more efficient way. In fact, Glance allows you to use the images as templates for new instances, take snapshots, and backups.

Glance is not a storage service for those images and can rely on multiple storage services, such as the OpenStack Object Storage Service. Due to this fact, Glance can be easily integrated with the current storage architecture and can contain a large number of images, based on the amount of free space available in your backend storage.

Glance provides a REST API interface to integrate with other components to allow other components to manage (indirectly) machines, images, and templates.

Glance can be compared to Amazon's **Amazon Machine Image (AMI)** system.

OpenStack Dashboard – Horizon

Horizon is the OpenStack dashboard and can help users to handle OpenStack resources without the need for command-line access. Horizon has been added in Essex, the fifth release of OpenStack.

Horizon is a web interface for OpenStack and all components of OpenStack can be managed in Horizon. This allows OpenStack end users to access their account and to manage their OpenStack resources without the need of a system administrator and of connecting via terminal to the cluster. This improves OpenStack security.

Horizon is designed to allow easy integration with other products and services, in order to allow an easy deployment and usage with third-party software.

Horizon can be compared to Amazon's **AWS Management Console**.

OpenStack Identity Service – Keystone

Keystone is the identity server of OpenStack. It has been added to OpenStack in Essex.

Keystone is a service that catalogs the available API endpoints and allows a centralization of user permissions in OpenStack. Due to the high sensibility of these information, it will be very costly and unsafe to let each component manage them. To do so, Keystone keeps all information in a secure way and all the other components that need them will be able to access it using the Keystone REST API. Keystone allows multiple authentication methods such as username and password, token-based system and **Amazon Web Services** (**AWS**) login.

Keystone supports multiple backends to store this data, such as LDAP.

Keystone can be compared to Amazon's **AWS Identity and Access Management** (**IAM**).

OpenStack Networking Service – Neutron

In Folsom (the sixth release of OpenStack), a networking module called Quantum has been added. Due to some branding issues, since Havana (the eighth OpenStack release), this module has been renamed as Neutron.

Neutron allows you to create and manage virtual networking in an easy yet powerful way. It allows to have global networks that are valid for all users and managed by administrators and user networks that are usable and manageable by a single user. In the case of user networks, the network will be visible and usable only by that specific user.

Neutron does not only provide basic networking, but also provides advanced networking tools, such as floating IPs. Also, it provides an extension framework allowing the deployment and management of other network services such as **Intrusion Detection Systems (IDS)**, load balancers, firewalls, and virtual private networks (VPN). For administrators, there is the possibility to use **software-defined networking (SDN)** technology such as OpenFlow to support multitenancy and horizontal scaling.

Neutron can be compared to Amazon's **Amazon Virtual Private Cloud (VPC)**.

OpenStack Block Storage Service – Cinder

Cinder is a Block Storage for OpenStack. It has been included in OpenStack since Folsom (the sixth release of OpenStack).

Cinder is able to provide block-level storage devices to Nova. Cinder interface and its features are comparable to the block storage providers available in commercial SAN products, so any user is able to create, manage, and use their block storage devices. Cinder does support multiple backends, such as Ceph, GlusterFS, NFS, and multiple proprietary SAN systems.

Cinder can be compared to Amazon's **Amazon Elastic Block Store (EBS)**.

OpenStack Orchestration – Heat

Heat has been a part of OpenStack since Havana (the eighth release of OpenStack). It can be used to orchestrate cloud applications using templates, and to automatically create machines on demand.

Heat can be used to create machines on demand from templates to allow an application to grow horizontally without any need for direct commands from the administrators.

To help the administrators that have to manage multiple infrastructure on OpenStack and Amazon, or are migrating the infrastructure from Amazon to OpenStack, Heat does support Amazon CloudFormation template syntax.

Heat can be compared to Amazon's **Amazon CloudFormation**.

OpenStack Telemetry – Ceilometer

Ceilometer has been added to OpenStack in Havana (the eighth release of OpenStack) with Heat, since they are complementary. In fact, Ceilometer provides data about the user's usage of resources, so as to be able to bill the people based on the actual resources used.

Ceilometer provides a single service that centralizes each service counter, so it's possible to export the usage data that will be needed to calculate the customer billing. All data available in Ceilometer are traceable and the whole process can be audited. Ceilometer data can also help companies using OpenStack in their private cloud to understand which processes and Business Units use more resources.

Ceilometer can be compared to Amazon's **Amazon CloudWatch**.

OpenStack Database Service – Trove

Trove is a database-as-a-service that is able to provide databases that are both relational and nonrelational. It has been added in Icehouse (the ninth release of OpenStack) and has been heavily improved in Juno (the tenth release of OpenStack).

Trove manages the database for the user, so it's capable of migrating a database from a machine to another or to scale the machine size based on the required resources. It also provides a RESTful API to communicate to the databases to completely abstract the database and its management. Also, the native interface of the chosen database is always available. Currently, it supports relational databases such as MySQL, NoSQL databases such as MongoDB, Cassandra, Redis, CouchDB, CouchBase, and in-memory databases such as MemCached and VoltDB.

Trove can be compared to Amazon's **Amazon Relational Database Service (RDS)**, but Amazon's service only supports relational databases.

OpenStack Data Processing Service – Sahara

Sahara is a Hadoop-as-a-service system. It's very new; in fact, it has been added in Juno (the tenth release).

Sahara allows the user to create Hadoop clusters quickly and easily. It also allows the user to be fully in control of the clusters, being able to set a lot of settings such as Hadoop version, cluster topology, and node's hardware details. After the user completes this information, Sahara deploys the cluster in a few minutes.

Sahara also allows the user to launch and manage MapReduce jobs on the clusters that have created.

Sahara can be compared to Amazon's **Amazon Elastic MapReduce (EMR)**.

Future components

Since the OpenStack community is increasing its size very quickly, the OpenStack Technical Committee has created a procedure to accept new components as part of OpenStack.

To grant maximum safety and code-continuity, it has been decided that the new components have to pass a given time in incubation. In this period, the component has to show a few releases as if they were already parts of OpenStack before they can be promoted to official components. This makes the incubation process pretty long but you can be assured that only high quality components are allowed to be officially part of OpenStack.

Due to this long process, we already know that some components that will soon become part of OpenStack. The following components are being considered to be part of the next release (Kilo) and some of them will very likely be integrated. These components are explained next.

Ironic – bare metal provisioning

The ironic goal is to provide the same interface that is used to create virtual instances in OpenStack to create real (bare metal) machines as well. The main goal of this is to help a system administrator to centralize the administration of the machines.

Amazon does not provide any service that is comparable to Ironic.

Zaqar – cloud messaging

Zaqar is a cloud messaging service for web developers. The service features a RESTful API, which developers can use to send messages between various components of their software and mobile applications. During the early phase of the development of Zaqar, it was known as **Marconi**, but since has been renamed.

Zaqar can be compared to Amazon's **Amazon Simple Queue Service (SQS)** service, but with the additional support for event broadcasting. Also, some features of Zaqar can be found in Amazon's **Amazon Simple Notification Service (SNS)**.

Manila – file sharing

Manila is a file sharing service provider. Manila volumes are accessible as NFS and CIFS volumes, as well as through the RESTful interface. Manila also supports ACL at the file level. It can use GlusterFS, NetApp, and IBM GPFS volumes as backends.

Manila can be compared to Amazon's **AWS Storage Gateway**.

Designate – DNS

Designate is a DNS-as-a-service provider. It is able to manage multiple DNS instances for redundancy reasons and to keep them all synchronized properly. Multiple backends can be used such as PowerDNS, NSD4, FreeIPA, DynECT, and BIND9.

Designate can be compared to Amazon's **Amazon Route 53**.

Barbican – key management

Barbican is a key (secrets) manager for OpenStack. Barbican handles many types of secrets, including:

- Symmetric keys that can be used to encrypt Swift containers and Cinder block storages
- Asymmetric keys that can be used for secure communications such as SSL/TLS, encrypted e-mails, and SSH
- Raw secrets that can be used to keep secure data in Barbican

Barbican can be compared to Amazon's **AWS Key Management Service (KMS)**.

Summary

In this chapter, we have seen the differences between private and public cloud with a specific focus on security, the different kind of attackers, and attacks with a focus on cloud computing, as well as the components of OpenStack.

In the next chapter, we will focus on networking security for OpenStack.

3
Securing OpenStack Networking

OpenStack, as any other software, has to assume certain hypothesis as though they were true. This is necessary to develop flexible software in a speedy way. On the other side of the coin, this approach endangers the security of the software. In the case of OpenStack, there is a single hypothesis that can trash your security measurements.

 OpenStack fully trusts each node of the cluster.

As we have seen in the *Hypervisor breakout* section in *Chapter 2, OpenStack Security Challenges*, this exposes all the data and resources in the cluster in case someone obtains access to a machine in the cluster. The hypervisor breakout is not the only case in which this can happen, and is rare. The most common exploit of that hypothesis is a network attack in which the attacker is able to use an insecure network to gain access to more data than it should.

The Open Systems Interconnection model

In 1984, ISO/IEC 7498-1 was published, which defines the **Open Systems Interconnection (OSI)** model. The OSI model is a theoretical model to divide a communication between two machines in abstraction layers.

 Even if the OSI model is not used in the real world, it is critical, because it helps you to understand the networking communications and their implications clearly. Also, very often, those layers are referred to in networking, in phrases such as "we got a problem on layer 3".

The OSI model consists of the following seven layers:

1. Physical
2. Data link
3. Network
4. Transport
5. Session
6. Presentation
7. Application

Layer 1 – the Physical layer

This is the lowest layer and it relates the physical part, as the name suggests. This layer cares about bit stream, so it will be electrical, light, or radio impulses.

The following are the standards that fall in this layer:

- IEEE 802.11a/b/g/n/ac (WiFi)10BASE-T
- 100BASE-TX
- 1000BASE T
- 10GBASE T
- 40GBASE-T (Ethernet standards over RJ-45 twisted pair of copper cables) **Synchronous Optical Networking (SONET)**
- **Synchronous Digital Hierarchy (SDH)** (common optical fiber standards)

The physical layer standards define the basic things about the cables and connectors, such as the layout of pins, line impedance, voltages, cable specifications, connectors' shapes, and many other similar things.

If a colleague comes to you saying that he thinks there is a layer 1 problem, means that he thinks either the cable or the ports are faulty.

As for security, layer 1 attacks are the ones that see the attacker messing directly with the cables. The two possible attacks aim respectively to a denial-of-service and to data duplication.

In the first case, the attacker would cut or unplug a cable to inhibit two machines to communicate. An example of this could be an attacker that identifies the network cable exiting your data center and cuts it to make all the data available in your data center unavailable to the outside world.

In the second case, the attacker would somehow copy all the data passing through your cable to another cable to be able to collect and parse them. An example of this case could be an attacker who cuts a cable in a moment when no one would be checking, crimps connectors to both the pieces, and adds some hardware in between, such as a passive LAN tap, to be able to read all data streaming through the cable without being discovered.

Layer 2 – the Data link layer

By moving up one level in the networking stack, we can find the data link. This layer deals with frames that are bits with a source and a destination. In this layer, the source and destination addresses are the **Media Access Control** (**MAC**) addresses. Data can be passed from the source to the destination only if they are in the same network, so they don't have any router or firewall in the middle.

In this layer, a lot of low-level operation occurs such as error control, flow control, spanning tree mitigation with **Spanning Tree Protocol** (**STP**) or its evolutions, **Quality of Service** (**QoS**) control, and **Virtual LANs** (**VLAN**).

So, a layer 2 problem usually means something related to MAC addresses, STP, and VLAN that went wrong.

From a security prospect, layer 2 is crucial, because a lot of sensible data passes in this level such as broadcast announcements and requests. If the network is deployed properly, you will have a router or a firewall on any connection that goes outside your walls, even if that line is yours or dedicated. In this case, to be able to do a layer 2 attack, the attacker has to be physically in your building or be able to connect to a machine in your building.

Multiple kinds of attacks are possible in layer 2, the most common ones are the following:

- **Address Resolution Protocol (ARP)** spoofing
- MAC flooding and **Content Addressable Memory (CAM)** table overflow attack
- **Dynamic Host Configuration Protocol (DHCP)** starvation attack
- **Cisco Discovery Protocol (CDP)** attacks
- STP attacks
- **Virtual LAN (VLAN)** attacks

This list only counts for cabled networks, because Wi-Fi networking has all those plus many more attack vehicles, but since the Wi-Fi technology is not used in the server farm, those problems are excluded from our goal.

Address Resolution Protocol (ARP) spoofing

ARP is a protocol that allows identification of the MAC address of a machine by its IP. To improve its performances, historically, every machine listens for ARP packages and updates their ARP tables every time a host affirms that it owns an IP and a MAC address even if no ARP request has been issued.

ARP spoofing is an attack that allows an attacker to make the other host in the network thinks he is someone else sending out a crafted ARP package with the machine's real MAC and another machine IP. The most common type of attack is the attacker faking to be the gateway to be able to perform a **Man in the Middle (MitM)** attack. The single most effective way to prevent this is to enable the port security feature on your switches.

 Hubs are simple signal replicators and should be avoided in any situation. Always use switches instead of hubs.

MAC flooding and Content Addressable Memory table overflow attack

To improve their performances, all switches maintain a CAM table that lists all known MAC addresses with the indication of which port to use to reach them. This allows the switch to send a package for a specific MAC address, only to the port where that MAC address is connected. MAC flooding attack aims to saturate the CAM table of the switch. To do so, the attacker will fake many Ethernet frames from random MAC addresses and those will be sent to the switch. The switch will add all those new MAC addresses to its CAM table, and in the end the CAM table will be saturated.

 If a switch has the CAM table full, it will act as if it was a hub, relaying all data to all ports, so any computer connected to that switch with the packet analyzer software will be able to log all traffic passing through the switch itself.

To prevent this kind of attack, you need to enable the port security feature and to limit the number of MAC address that can be authorized on a single physical port. The best way to prevent this kind of attack would be to deactivate the MAC autodiscovery, but this can scale out badly because every time you add, change, move, or remove a box you'll have to update the switch configuration.

Dynamic Host Configuration Protocol (DHCP) starvation attack

The majority of networks today have the DHCP enabled to distribute IP addresses, gateway addresses, and DNS addresses without the need for any manual configuration. Every time a MAC address requests an IP to a DHCP server, the DHCP server will reply with an IP address. In the DHCP starvation attack, the attacker will perform thousands of IP requests until the DHCP server runs out of assignable IPs. At this point, if new clients try to request an IP address, the DHCP server will not be able to provide them anymore and the new clients will not be able to navigate properly, so a DoS has been performed. There is another possible outcome to this attack, that is, if the attacker does create a new (rogue) DHCP server, which has free IPs. If this happens, the new clients will ask for an IP address and the rogue DHCP server will assign them properly. Since the IPs of gateways and DNS are also provided by the DHCP server, the rogue DHCP server can provide its IP as the gateway, so it will be able to perform a MitM attack on those clients.

The best way to mitigate this kind of attack is to enable port security and to limit the maximum number of MAC address for each physical port. In fact, if you set 10 MAC addresses for each physical port, the attacker will be able to steal only 10 addresses from your DHCP, if he is able to access a single physical connector.

Cisco Discovery Protocol (CDP) attacks

The CDP is enabled by default on all Cisco devices and allows them to coordinate themselves. CDP is an unauthenticated and clear text protocol, so it has no embedded securities. This is a Cisco proprietary protocol, so only if you have at least one Cisco device in your infrastructure, you can be affected by this. The CDP aims to make possible a communication (and coordination) of the multiple Cisco devices you probably have on your network.

There are multiple attacks that can be performed against this protocol, including the following:

- Denial-of-service that will inhibit the attacked hardware to work at all
- Cache overflow that allows the routers/switches to reset to fabric conditions
- Power exhaustion that will leave your switches without enough energy to run properly, exploiting the reserve electrical power feature created for VoIP devices
- Cache pollution that will make the usefulness of CDP disappear, since its tables will be full of garbage making them useless

To prevent and mitigate those attacks, we have various options. The safest one is to deactivate the CDP on any Cisco hardware. However even if this is a safe way to prevent these kinds of attacks, you probably have reasons to want those protocols in your organization since it helps network admins. A middle ground option is to disable the CDP on all ports that have clients on them, leaving it enabled only on ports between networking devices.

Spanning Tree Protocol (STP) attacks

STP is a very common technology to be found on networks. Its goal is to grant in any given moment that no loops are possible in the network. To do so, it uses **Bridge Protocol Data Units** (**BPDU**), which are special packages crafted to detect loops. This protocol assumes trust between networking appliances. This opens up the way for multiple attacks like the following:

- Sending configuration BPDU, with this kind of attack, is possible to inform all layer 2 switches that a new configuration is available

- Sending **Topology Change Notification** (**TCN**) BPDU, in this case, it's possible to fake the addition, or elimination of a node

- Claiming Root Role, in this kind of attack, the attacker informs all other nodes to be the Root switch and so a lot of traffic will pass through it

- Claiming Other Role, in this case, the attacker can claim to be in a certain position of the tree, and therefore is able to capture specific traffic, knowing some information about the network

As you can see, there are a lot of different ways to exploit STP. The basic rule to make STP safe is to disable it from any interface that is not used to connect switches together. Also, on many important vendors' switches, you can enable root guard or BPDU guard to mitigate these kind of attacks.

Virtual LAN (VLAN) attacks

VLAN attacks are nowadays present in all complex networks since they are an economical way to split different systems in multiple networks without having to buy multiple switches. The VLAN protocol is standardized in the IEEE 802.1Q document. VLAN works thanks to an additional header added to each package (also known as VLAN header or 802.1Q header) that identifies the VLAN the package is a part of. On Cisco devices, VLAN can be managed using the Cisco proprietary **VLAN Trunking Protocol** (**VTP**), a protocol that allows centralized management of VLAN instead of management for each network appliance. OpenStack Quantum can use VLAN, so we will speak more about VLAN and L2 tunnels later in this chapter.

VLAN is susceptible to the following attacks:

- VTP attack: In this kind of attack, the attacker will send VTP packages with changes to VLANs. If the switches read and apply those changes, the attacker will be able to do anything he wants with your VLANs.

- VLAN hopping attack: In this case, the attacker will make your network believe it is a switch and subscribe to more VLANs than it should, being able in this way to access those new VLANs.

- Double encapsulation: In this case, the attacker puts two 802.1Q headers in each package, his own and the victim's. If the switch has the port set for negotiation, the package will be sent to the victim's VLAN.

There are multiple exploits that allow the attacker to somehow escape from the VLAN or to mess with your VLANs. To prevent and mitigate those attacks, you can do the following:

- Always use a dedicated VLAN for the trunks port, so double tagging is harder
- Disable unused ports and put them in an unused VLAN, so even if someone can enable them, it will be of no use
- Don't use VLAN 1 for any use, since some switches can interpret VLAN 1 as untagged traffic
- Disable trunking on ports that are not switch facing, so it's not possible for an attacker to fake being a switch
- Use 802.1Q tags on all ports
- Disable VTP or at least force basic security (such as MD5 authentication)

Layer 3 – the Network layer

Moving up one level in the networking stack, we can find the network link. This is the last layer classified as media layer, since it's the last layer that is directly managed by your networking infrastructure. This layer deals with packages. In this layer, the source and destination addresses are **Internet Protocol (IP)** either version 4 or 6. The data can move from a network to another using routers and layer 3 switches.

In this layer, all high-level networking occurs, such as **Internet Protocol Security (IPSec)**, **Internet Control Message Protocol (ICMP)**, and **Internet Group Management Protocol (IGMP)**. Multiple protocols can be used for routing; the most common ones are **Open Shortest Path First (OSPF)**, **Routing Information Protocol (RIP)**, **Enhanced Interior Gateway Routing Protocol (EIGRP)**, and **Border Gateway Protocol (BGP)**.

From a security perspective, there are two major attacks that can be performed at this level:

- ICMP DDoS attack, such as smurf attacks and ping flood
- Exploit the routing protocol to execute a MitM attack

Layer 4 – the Transport layer

The transport layer provides the ability to move variable-length data sequences from a source host to a destination host. This is the first time for the host layer since the switches and routers will not interfere with it and the data will make sense only to the sender and to the receiver. Today this is not completely true because we have stately firewalls, but this was true in the past.

The most common technologies found in this layer are **Transmission Control Protocol (TCP)** and **User Datagram Protocol (UDP)**.

From a security standpoint, the most probable attack is a DDoS pointing to a badly handled exception of the TCP stack, such as the SYN flood attack. For these kinds of threats, you should use the **Intrusion prevention systems (IPS)** with the **Network behavior analysis (NBA)** feature.

Layer 5 – the Session layer

The session layer is in charge of the connection between the two hosts. Its role is to establish, terminate, and manage the connections between the two hosts. It can setup different kinds of connections, such as half-duplex, full-duplex, and simplex.

The most common example of layer 5 is the TCP socket.

The most dangerous attack at this level is session hijacking. In this kind of attack, the attacker will retrieve information about an active and legitimate session and impersonate the client to be able to receive data from the server. The best way to prevent that kind of attack is encrypting all data using **Transport Layer Security (TLS)**.

Layer 6 – the Presentation layer

The presentation layer is in charge of transforming the data from the application formats to the networks format. It formats and encrypts the data before sending it to lower layers, and for this reason, it is also called the **syntax layer**.

The currently most well-known example of technology at this layer is the TLS.

This layer is critical for the security of the applications, and many times attackers have tried breaching TLS or other similar technology. An example is the Heartbleed vulnerability discovered in OpenSSL during April 2014. The best way to secure yourself from these kinds of attacks is to keep your system up-to-date and to check your configurations; in fact, the majority of the problems at this layer come from 0 days and misconfigurations.

Layer 7 – the Application layer

The application layer is the highest one, and therefore, the closest to the user. This layer interacts with applications that communicate using networking.

The examples of technology at this layer are well known, such as **Hypertext Transfer Protocol (HTTP)**, **File Transfer Protocol (FTP)**, **Simple Mail Transfer Protocol (SMTP)**, **Domain Name System (DNS)**, **Network File System (NFS)**, **Network Time Protocol (NTP)**, and many others.

As for the security, in the application layer, we have very similar problems and solutions to the 6th layer, which is the presentation layer.

TCP/IP

The OSI Model, even if it is very popular and very important to understand how networking works, is not used in the real world, since Internet and all networks we usually use are based on the TCP/IP stack. The TCP/IP stack has fewer layers and it is pretty straight forward when you know the OSI Model. Let's take a look at the following diagram:

	OSI	TCP/IP
7	Application	Applications (FTP, SMTP, HTTP, etc.)
6	Presentation	
5	Session	
4	Transport	TCP (host-to-host)
3	Network	IP
2	Data link	Network access (usually Ethernet)
1	Physical	

Architecting secure networks

On top of what we have already seen until now about the network security, we need to remember a couple more rules as well, which are as follows:

- Different uses means different network
- The importance of the **Intrusion Detection System (IDS)** and **Intrusion Prevention System (IPS)**

Different uses means different network

This best practice involves dividing into different networks (usually using VLANs) for different kinds of data. This is a best practice that very often people ignore because is easier to manage flat networks than more structured network.

The advantages of this approach are multiple and in the following sectors:

- Security
- Redundancy
- Performance
- Scalability

Let's start from the last one listed, since it is the easiest to analyze. Very often you create a network with the idea of adding few servers, but later you'll find yourself adding more servers to the same network. At the end, you'll end up needing to add a machine, but you'll have no IP address to assign to the machine. How did this happen? Often people assign a 24 IP class to a network, which has only 254 usable addresses. Even if this number seems huge at the beginning, later it will seem too small. The real problem is that if you want to change the class, you'll have to change it on a huge number of machines.

Performance-wise, if you have huge networks with hundreds (or thousands) of machines, you'll see thousands of broadcast messages that will hit all your machines every time. Clearly, every machine will immediately drop all the packages that are not interesting for them, but this will use up your bandwidth.

As for redundancy, this is connected to the redundancy systems that are possible on the various networking layers. If you have a huge flat network, you'll have the biggest part of communications at layer 2 because the machines will often be in the same network of the machine they want to communicate with, so they will use Mac addresses instead of IPs. It's possible to make a redundant layer 2 network, but it is expensive and the expenses grow directly with the increase of the redundancy level and number of machines you own.

Redundancy in layer 2 is obviously necessary in either case, but can be minimized in a segmented network environment preferring the much cheaper and better scaling layer 3 redundancy.

Security is also a huge reason to trash a flat network design. Let's start from a classic example, we have a reverse proxy, an application server that needs a MySQL server, and an NFS, as shown in the following figure:

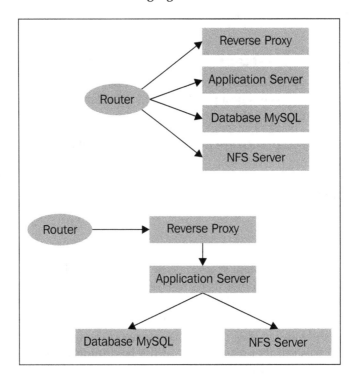

 We are intentionally ignoring redundancy for simplicity and clarity.

As we can see, in the preceding figure, if the attacker is able to breach in the reverse proxy machine, he can directly attack the MySQL and the NFS servers. In the second case, he has to attack before the Application Server then can attack the MySQL and NFS systems. This slows down the attacker. Also, consider that in a flat network scenario, you'll very often have machines with different systems in the same network, so if one system is compromised, the attacker can try to attack all machines in the network, instead of the few machines logically connected to it.

Also, you have to remember that if an attacker is able to take control of a machine connected to a network, he will be able to perform layer 2 attacks to be able to spoof all data in the network. Encrypted data is safer, but still a lot of data move unencrypted.

The importance of firewall, IDS, and IPS

The security of a network can and should be achieved in multiple ways. Three components that are critical to the security of a network are:

- Firewall
- Intrusion detection system (IDS)
- Intrusion prevention system (IPS)

Firewall

Firewalls are systems that control traffic passing through them based on rules. This can seem something like a router, but they are very different. The router allows communication between different networks while the firewall limits communication between networks and hosts. The root of this confusion may occur because very often the router will have the firewall functionality and vice versa.

[Firewalls need to be connected in a series to your infrastructure.]

The first paper on the firewall technology appeared in 1988 and designed the **packet filter** firewall. This kind of firewall is often known as **first generation firewall**. This kind of firewall analyzes the packages passing through and if the package matches a rule, the firewall will act accordingly to that rule. This firewall will analyze each package by itself and will not consider other aspects such as other packages. It works on the first three layers of the OSI model with very few features using layer 4 specifically to check port numbers and protocols (UDP/TCP). First generation firewalls are still in use, because in a lot of situations, to do the job properly and are cheap and secure. Examples of typical filtering those firewalls prohibit (or allow) to IPs of certain classes (or specific IPs), to access certain IPs, or allow traffic to a specific IP only on specific ports. There are no known attacks to those kind of firewalls, but specific models can have specific bugs that can be exploited.

In 1990, a new generation of firewall appeared. The initial name was **circuit-level gateway**, but today it is far more commonly known as **stateful firewalls** or **second generation firewall**. These firewalls are able to understand when connections are being initialized and closed so that the firewall comes to know what is the current state of a connection when a package arrives. To do so, this kind of firewall uses the first four layers of the networking stack. This allows the firewall to drop all packages that are not establishing a new connection or are in an already established connection. These firewalls are very powerful with the TCP protocol because it has states, while they have very small advantages compared to first generation firewalls handling UDP or ICMP packages, since those packages travel with no connection. In these cases, the firewall sets the connection as established; only the first valid package passes through and closes it after the connection times out. Performance-wise, stateful firewall can be faster than packet firewall because if the package is part of an active connection, no further test will be performed against that package. These kinds of firewalls are more susceptible to bugs in their code since reading more about the package makes it easier to exploit. Also, on many devices, it is possible to open connections (with SYN packages) until the firewall is saturated. In such cases, the firewall usually downgrades itself as a simple router allowing all traffic to pass through it.

In 1991, improvements were made to the stateful firewall allowing it to understand more about the protocol of the package it was evaluating. The firewalls of this kind before 1994 had major problems, such as working as a proxy that the user had to interact with. In 1994, the first **application firewall**, as we know it, was born doing all its job completely transparently. To be able to understand the protocol, this kind of firewall requires an understanding of all seven layers of the OSI model. As for security, the same as the stateful firewall does apply to the application firewall as well.

Intrusion detection system (IDS)

IDSs are systems that monitor the network traffic looking for policy violation and malicious traffic.

 The goal of the IDS is not to block malicious activity, but instead to log and report them.

These systems act in a passive mode, so you'll not see any traffic coming from them. This is very important because it makes them invisible to attackers so you can gain information about the attack, without the attacker knowing.

 IDSs need to be connected in parallel to your infrastructure.

Intrusion prevention system (IPS)

IPSs are sometimes referred to as **Intrusion Detection and Prevention Systems (IDPS)**, since they are IDS that are also able to fight back malicious activities. IPSs have greater possibility to act than IDSs. Other than reporting, like IDS, they can also drop malicious packages, reset the connection, and block the traffic from the offending IP address.

 IPSs need to be connected in series to your infrastructure.

Generic Routing Encapsulation (GRE)

GRE is a Cisco tuning protocol that is difficult to position in the OSI model. The best place for it to be is between layers 2 and 3. Being above layer 2 (where VLANs are), we can use GRE inside VLAN. We will not go deep into the technicalities of this protocol. I'd like to focus more on the advantages and disadvantages it has over VLAN.

The first advantage of (extended) GRE over VLAN is scalability. In fact, VLAN is limited to 4,096, while GRE tunnels do not have this limitation. If you are running a private cloud and you are working in a small corporation, 4,096 networks could be enough, but will definitely not be enough if you work for a big corporation or if you are running a public cloud. Also, unless you use VTP for your VLANs, you'll have to add VLANs to each network device, while GREs don't need this.

 You cannot have more than 4,096 VLANs in an environment.

The second advantage is security. Since you can deploy multiple GRE tunnels in a single VLAN, you can connect a machine to a single VLAN and multiple GRE networks without the risks that come with putting a port in trunking that is needed to bring more VLANs in the same physical port.

For these reasons, GRE has been a very common choice in a lot of OpenStack clusters deployed up to OpenStack Havana. The current preferred networking choice (since Icehouse) is **Virtual Extensible LAN (VXLAN)**.

VXLAN

VXLAN is a network virtualization technology whose specifications have been originally created by Arista Networks, Cisco, and VMWare, and many other companies have backed the project. Its goal is to offer a standardized overlay encapsulation protocol and it was created because the standard VLAN were too limited for the current cloud needs and the GRE protocol was a Cisco protocol.

It works using layer 2 Ethernet frames within layer 4 UDP packages on port 4789.

As for the maximum number of networks, the limit is 16 million logical networks.

Since the Icehouse release, the suggested standard for networking is VXLAN.

Flat network versus VLAN versus GRE in OpenStack Quantum

In OpenStack Quantum, you can decide to use multiple technologies for your networks: flat network, VLAN, GRE, and the most recent, VXLAN. Let's discuss them in detail:

- **Flat network**: It is often used in private clouds since it is very easy to set up. The downside is that any virtual machine will see any other virtual machines in our cloud. I strongly discourage people from using this network design because it's unsafe, and in the long run, it will have problems, as we have seen earlier.

- **VLAN**: It is sometimes used in bigger private clouds and sometimes even in small public clouds. The advantage is that many times you already have a VLAN-based installation in your company. The major disadvantages are the need to trunk ports for each physical host and the possible problems in propagation. I discourage this approach, since in my opinion, the advantages are very limited while the disadvantages are pretty strong.

- **VXLAN**: It should be used in any kind of cloud due to its technical advantages. It allows a huge number of networks, its way more secure, and often eases debugging.

- **GRE**: Until the Havana release, it was the suggested protocol, but since the Icehouse release, the suggestion has been to move toward VXLAN, where the majority of the development is focused.

Design a secure network for your OpenStack deployment

As for the physical infrastructure, we have to design it securely. We have seen that the network security is critical and that there a lot of possible attacks in this realm. Is it possible to design a secure environment to run OpenStack? Yes it is, if you remember a few rules:

- Create different networks, at the very least for management and external data (this network usually already exists in your organization and is the one where all your clients are)
- Never put ports on trunking mode if you use VLANs in your infrastructure, otherwise physically separated networks will be needed

The following diagram is an example of how to implement it:

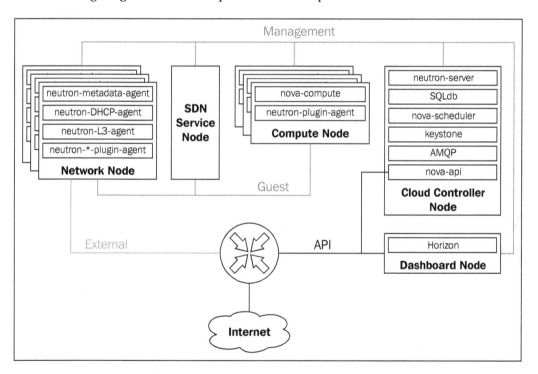

Here, the management, tenant external networks could be either VLAN or real networks. Remember that to not use VLAN trunking, you need at least the same amount of physical ports as of VLAN, and the machine has to be subscribed to avoid port trunking that can be a huge security hole.

A management network is needed for the administrator to administer the machines and for the OpenStack services to speak to each other. This network is critical, since it may contain sensible data, and for this reason, it has to be disconnected from other networks, or if not possible, have very limited connectivity.

The external network is used by virtual machines to access the Internet (and vice versa). In this network, all machines will need an IP address reachable from the Web.

The tenant network, sometimes even called internal or guest network is the network where the virtual machines can communicate with other virtual machines in the same cloud. This network, in some deployment cases, can be merged with the external network, but this choice has some security drawbacks.

The API network is used to expose OpenStack APIs to the users. This network requires IP addresses reachable from the Web, and for this reason, is often merged into the external network.

There are cases where provider networks are needed to connect tenant networks to existing networks outside the OpenStack cluster. Those networks are created by the OpenStack administrator and map directly to an existing physical network in the data center.

The networking resource policy engine

In OpenStack, there are a lot of policy files that can help you tune the default policies to meet your specific needs. If you are using Red Hat or CentOS, you can find the OpenStack Networking policy file in /etc/neutron/policy.json.

Virtual Private Network as a Service (VPNaaS)

As we have already seen, it's very important to encrypt everything, and even more if your traffic passes through third parties or shared networks. Since you might need to connect some external resources (such as servers in a remote location or your laptop to do some configuration) to your tenant network, OpenStack Networking allows you to create VPN end points in a few clicks or commands.

This is very useful if you use some unsafe protocols. If you will use only safe protocols such as SSH and HTTPS, you can still use a VPN if you want to be sure that no one will be able to even collect metadata of your communications.

Summary

In this chapter, we have seen how networking works, which attacks we can expect, and how we can counter them. Also, we have seen how to implement a secure deployment of OpenStack Networking.

In the next chapter, we'll see how we can harden OpenStack communications and APIs.

4
Securing OpenStack Communications and Its API

In our world, where the majority of transactions of money, goods, and information are executed over the Internet, the importance of encryption is becoming critical.

In this chapter, we will dive into encryption and hashing to understand the capabilities of and possible security threats that these technologies can bring to you and your infrastructure. After this, we will see how the public key infrastructure works so you can understand the various weak points it can hide. Then, we will look at how to set up httpd and nginx with certificates to secure OpenStack APIs.

Encryption is a part of human history. Since the Roman emperor Gaius Julius Cesar (100–44 BC), many people have tried to create secure encryptions. The first attempt to create a cryptography system that is considered safe today was made by Frank Miller (1842–1925), who proposed one-time pads to enhance Vigenere encryption. Those pads created with random characters were used a single time to encrypt a message. An example could be as follows:

```
PLAIN TEXT:   HELLO WORLD
KEY:          BRYWD EMOVO
CIPHER TEXT:  IVJHR AAFGR
```

As you can see, with one-time pads, you can enable secure cryptography. Although it is unbreakable if correctly implemented, this kind of cipher is not used commonly since it has multiple drawbacks:

- The one-time pads have to be composed with truly random characters
- The one-time pads have to be exchanged
- The one-time pads have to be as long as the total combined length of all messages that are intended to be sent until the next pad exchange

These problems were partially solved by the German Army during World War II with Enigma. Enigma is a machine that encrypts and decrypts a text by identifying the positions of three rotors and a few patches. This allowed the German Army, particularly the U-boats, to have months of valid codes on a few sheets of paper. This obviously was way less secure than the perfect Vigenere cipher; in fact, it was breached during WWII.

After the World War II, a huge number of attempts to create secure encryption were made. We will see them as we go on in the chapter.

Encryption security

One of the most important things about encryption is security. This can seem to be obvious, but it's not.

> Different encryption techniques and algorithms have different security levels and could be susceptible to different attacks.

Symmetric encryption

As you may have noticed, up to now, we have talked of systems where by knowing the algorithm and the key, you can both encrypt and decrypt a message. This kind of encryption is known as **symmetric encryption**. The big advantage of this kind of encryption is that it is easy because it does not require complex math and much calculation to execute. On the other hand, it makes critical the key exchange moment and key management. In fact, the key has to be exchanged before the transmission can start between the parties, and it has to be done securely. As for the key management problem, since both parties know the same secret (in fact, this kind of cryptography is also called **shared secret**), if you have multiple people that have to communicate with each other, you will need $n(n-1)/2$ keys — this means that in a group of 20 people, you'll need 190 keys.

The following is the schema of a communication using a symmetric encryption.

Today, the types of symmetric encryption that are used are as follows:

- Stream cipher
- Block cipher

Stream cipher

All the encryption methods we talked about in this chapter preface are stream ciphers. This kind of encryption is not very safe, but allows very cheap implementation and allows you to send messages of unknown length. Stream ciphers are based on XOR (exclusive OR) operations.

The most known and used stream cipher algorithm is RC4, which is used in the important parts of society, like **Wired Equivalent Privacy (WEP)**, **Wi-Fi Protected Access (WPA)**, **Secure Sockets Layer (SSL)**, **Transport Layer Security (TLS)**, and many more protocols.

Block cipher

Block ciphers are more used than stream ciphers in software products. Block ciphers operate on fixed-size groups of bits (blocks). A common size is 64 bit.

To understand what this could mean with a very easy example, we can try a transposition cipher, such as the rail fence cipher. In this cipher, the plain text is written downwards and diagonally on successive lines (also known as rails—hence the name of the cipher). When the bottom line is reached, the text bumps at the end (also known as fence) and starts moving upwards. The same process applies to the top line. The message is then read in rows, not counting the empty spaces. The following example can clarify this better:

```
PLAIN TEXT: HELLO WORLD

LINE1: H...L...R..
LINE2: .E.L.O.O.L.
LINE3: ..L...W...D

CIPHER TEXT: HLREL OOLLWD
```

In this simple example, we have scrambled the text creating an anagram of the initial message. This is still somehow understandable since the text was very easy, but it gives you a good understanding of what a transposition cipher is.

Block ciphers have four ways to cipher data, which are as follows:

- **Confusion**: It is very complex relationships between the plaintext and the key that will prevent an attacker from determining the key altering the plain text
- **Diffusion**: This is a way to change the cipher text in multiple places every time the plain text is altered in a single place
- **Substitution**: This puts a different sign in place of the real one, such as substitution of a letter with another one
- **Transposition**: This scrambles the text, reordering it in a definite way, as in the rail fence cipher

These operations are usually simple, such as substitutions and permutations, but are executed in multiple rounds.

Since the strength of encryption is the number of attempts that are needed to break it, the encryption algorithm could be declared and made publicly available, and this would not make the encryption unsafe.

The first widespread block cipher is **Data Encryption Standard (DES)**. Today, DES is not used a lot since it has been proven too weak, while its improved version **Triple Data Encryption Standard (3DES or Triple DES)** is still used. Another important block cipher is **Advanced Encryption Standard (AES)**, which is probably today the most common block cipher algorithm.

Asymmetric encryption

Asymmetric encryption has some core differences from symmetric encryption. The first that you can immediately see is that in asymmetric encryption there are two keys: one public key to encrypt and a private key to decrypt. From this concept, one of the names of asymmetric encryption is derived: public key encryption. The process in an exchange of secure data with an asymmetric encryption is as seen here:

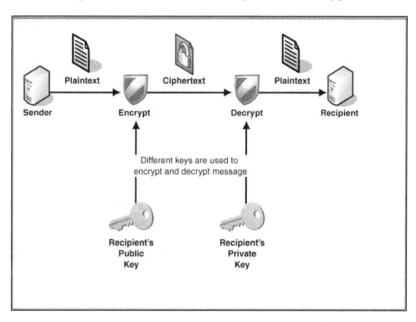

This approach does simplify greatly the key exchange and key management. For the key management, you only need a pair of keys (private/public) for each person. So if you have 20 people that have to communicate between themselves, you'll only need 20 pairs of keys. For the key exchange process, it becomes very easy since every user can share their public key online, and you only have to have the other person's public key to encrypt the message.

Also, asymmetric encryption allows you to sign messages, encrypting them with your private key, so that anyone with your private key can decrypt the message, understanding that it is coming from you and granting non-repudiation. The following figure shows this process:

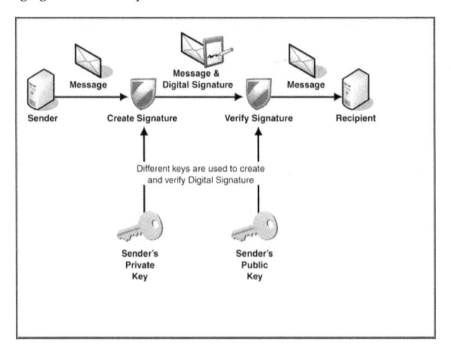

If you use asymmetric encryption to sign messages, its content will be available to anyone who knows your public key. That means that your message is not confidential. You can overcome this by signing the message with your private key and then encrypting it with the receiver key. By doing so, you are granted both confidentiality and non-repudiation.

Diffie-Hellman

Diffie-Hellman (also known as D-H or DH) was the first asymmetric algorithm and was released in 1976. It was named after its creators, Whitfield Diffie and Martin Hellman.

The Diffie-Hellman protocol works by using two constants: a **parameter** (p) and a **generator** (g). The parameter must be a prime number while the generator must be smaller than the parameter. Further, $gk = n \bmod p$ (where **k** is the key) has to apply for every **number** (n) from 1 to $p - 1$.

The Diffie-Hellman protocol security is granted by the **discrete logarithm problem**. This problem affirms that when there is a discrete logarithm, it is easy for a machine to solve it, but it's much more costly to find the original logarithm knowing only its result. The weak spot of the Diffie-Hellman algorithm is the key exchange because it does not require any authentication between the parties and, therefore, is vulnerable to man-in-the-middle attacks.

Today, the Diffie-Hellman algorithm is paired with authentication methods in many applications, such as the IPSec.

RSA algorithm

The year after the release of the Diffie-Hellman algorithm, Ron Rivest, Adi Shamir, and Leonard Adleman released a new algorithm for asymmetric encryption, the RSA, a name that has been derived from their initials.

RSA supports keys up to 4096 bits, and its security is based on the idea that it is hard to find the two factors that have been multiplied only knowing the result of the multiplication. This problem is also known as **prime factorization problem**. The real challenge for RSA is the randomness of the numbers necessary to create the key pair. In fact, if the numbers are not truly random, the whole algorithm could be insecure.

Due to the simplicity of the RSA algorithm, the complexity of the prime factorization problem, and the fact that the RSA patent expired in 2000, today RSA is the de facto standard for asymmetric encryption.

Elliptic Curve Cryptography

Elliptic Curve Cryptography (**ECC**) is based on the assumption that finding the discrete algorithm of a random elliptic curve element with respect to a publicly known base point is unfeasible.

The advantage of ECC is that you can have comparable security to a 3072-bit RSA with a 256-bit ECC. This means that low power devices can encrypt and decrypt ECC messages way faster than standard RSA messages.

Multiple methods of ECC have been established in the last few years, such as **Elliptic Curve Diffie-Hellman** (**ECDH**), **Elliptic Curve Digital Signature Algorithm** (**ECDSA**), and **Edwards-curve Digital Signature Algorithm** (**EdDSA**).

A few concerns have been raised about the security of ECC since the **National Security Agency (NSA)** has started to push strongly on ECC since 2005, arriving to push the **Dual Elliptic Curve Deterministic Random Bit Generation (Dual_EC_DRBG)** as a NIST national standard. In 2013, the Dual_EC_DRBG was proven intentionally weakened. From that moment, several companies like RSA and many others started to campaign against ECC, since it could be possible that other ECC standards have similar weaknesses.

Symmetric/asymmetric comparison and synergies

We have seen that symmetric and asymmetric encryption feature multiple differences. Let's recap these differences as follows:

Domain	Symmetric	Asymmetric
Able to grant	Confidential	Confidential, offering integrity, authentication, and non-repudiation
Needed key(s)	A single shared key	A public key and a private key
Key exchange	Complex and offline	Simple and online
Scalability	Not scalable, keys increase exponentially	Scalable
Key size	Small	Big
Implementation speed	Fast	Slow
Best for	Bulk data	Small amount of data, key exchange, digital envelopes, digital signatures, and digital certificate

As you can see, in multiple domains, symmetric and asymmetric keys are exact opposites. This means that they can be used together to fill each other's weaknesses. A way to do so is to create a **hybrid encryption** to initialize the communication using asymmetric encryption, and in this communication, exchange securely a key that will then be used to perform symmetric encryption on all the data that follows. This ensures the confidentiality, integrity, authentication, and non-repudiation of the communication granted by asymmetric encryption, and the high speed of data transfer granted by the speed of symmetric encryption.

Hashing

While encryption is about confidentiality, **hashing** is about integrity and authentication. Hashing algorithms reduce any amount of data to a fixed length value known as the hash value. This hash value is a sort of fingerprint of the initial data. Due to the algorithms used to create hash values, even small changes in the initial data will create huge changes in the hash value. This makes it harder to guess the initial data with a trial-and-error approach.

Since you can have initial data of the desired length, and the output will be of fixed length, there is the possibility that different initial data will have the same hash value. This is called **collision**.

For example, let's see the difference between `Password` and `password`:

```
$ echo "password" | shasum -a 1
c8fed00eb2e87f1cee8e90ebbe870c190ac3848c  -
$ echo "Password" | shasum -a 1
3f44a88d098cdb8a384922e88a30dbe67f7178fd  -
```

From a security standpoint, the biggest risk of hashing algorithms is the collisions. A well-designed algorithm should prevent collision; but the only way to create an algorithm that is collision-free would need a hash value longer than the text, making it pointless.

Hashing is a one-way algorithm, and it is not possible to extract the original data by knowing the hash value. For some hashing algorithms like MD5 that today have a huge number of collisions, you can simply Google a hash value, which will often give you a short string that matches that hash value. This does not mean that the original message that created that hash value will be the one you have found on Google, but often what you have found will be enough to create breaches in the security system you are dealing with.

You can use hashing to check if a file you have received is the same as the one that has been sent. You can also use it to check if a password given by the user is the right one to authenticate the user without really knowing the password, since you only stored the algorithm.

Downloading the example code

You can download the example code files for all Packt books you have purchased from your account at http://www.packtpub.com. If you purchased this book elsewhere, you can visit http://www.packtpub.com/support and register to have the files e-mailed directly to you.

MD5

MD5 is the most famous MD hashing algorithm and is one of the best-known of all hashing algorithms. It produces a 128-bit output (32 characters), processing the initial data in 512-bit blocks. You can use md5sum to see the MD5 hash value of a string in the following command:

```
$ echo "password" | md5sum
286755fad04869ca523320acce0dc6a4   -
```

 Today, MD5 is deprecated due to its high number of collisions. If you still use it, you should start migrating to new and more secure algorithms, such as SHA-2 or SHA-3.

SHA

The **Secure Hash Algorithm (SHA)** is another series of algorithms like MD5. The various algorithms that constitute the SHA series are:

- SHA-0: This is the first version of SHA and was withdrawn shortly after publication since a significant flaw was identified in the hashing algorithm itself.

- SHA-1: This produces 160-bit output (40 characters), and today it is considered at risk of breaking since it only offers 61 bits of security.

- SHA-2: This is a set of algorithms that can create outputs of 224-bit (56 characters), 256-bit (64 characters), 384-bit (96 characters), and 512-bit (128 characters). It's today considered safe since it can offer from 112 to 256 bits of security.

- SHA-3: This set of algorithms can create output like the SHA-2, but with an entirely different algorithm, which is based on the **Keccak algorithm**.

To see some examples of SHA hashing, we can do the following:

```
$ echo "password" | shasum -a 1
c8fed00eb2e87f1cee8e90ebbe870c190ac3848c   -
$ echo "password" | shasum -a 224
87c8cdddb2b4ea61c2d2752c24eb2e1f1ff05500173f504c4cda5291   -
$ echo "password" | shasum -a 256
```

```
6b3a55e0261b0304143f805a24924d0c1c44524821305f31d9277843b8a10f4e  -
$ echo "password" | shasum -a 384
ba5089942870d2d193bf4afaff72ac1aff6c683de523cb3e0346f85be55fef05786107
ab7af91d680e03a8a3357b6e77  -
$ echo "password" | shasum -a 512
9151440965cf9c5e07f81eee6241c042a7b78e9bb2dd4f928a8f6da5e369cdffdd2b70
c70663ee30d02115731d35f1ece5aad9b362aaa9850efa99e3d197212a  -
$ echo "password" | sha3sum -a 256
17eded3bf5ab67bb8e37295e3469e236888a7e53dc95cf744856a6419f4d0d48  -
$ echo "password" | sha3sum -a 384
96d331c664090bcf96a67aa438d7800f490c12fa5885c3e02197e2a8471c04dcbd78189
39e83f7f3084628922a088421  -
$ echo "password" | sha3sum -a 512
80200973224a3ab9855a99200c7404d2b33e87cc765497e86a9cfe5e202171bfb93608f
7539de7ffe0ac79f2e8ea4f7da616d4ff156178718152c9916ee77149  -
```

Public key infrastructure

As we have seen, all encryption methods require a handshaking phase before the actual transmission to decide the the algorithms and keys to be used. This is probably the single most risky moment of the whole communication. In fact, today the majority of hackers direct their efforts at breaking this initial communication. The single biggest challenge in this phase is to be sure that you are talking directly to the person/machine you want to talk to, and you don't have anything in the middle performing a man-in-the-middle attack. If you know the other party, it is a straightforward procedure since you already have the other party's public key. On the other hand, if you do not know the other party, you should be able to trust that the other party is really who they claim to be. An example of a daily situation where this happens is when you want to reach a website for the first time. To solve this, the **Public key infrastructure** (**PKI**) is needed.

The PKI allows two parties to communicate securely even if they did not know each other before. There are other ways to solve this problem, but the only one that concerns us in the study of OpenStack Security is the PKI with a centralized **Certify Authority** (**CA**).

The basic idea behind the centralized CA model is that there are one or few CA trusted by everyone and that grant that the certificate holder is trustable. This model is the base of the current implementation of SSL and TLS.

The best analogy I've ever heard for the PKI was told to me by a consultant working in the same company as I was. He compared the PKI to the passport system. In the passport system, every country has a person (the Prime Minister, the President, the King, and so on) that is trusted by the other countries. He cannot issue all passports and, so, has an office doing so. Since the people cannot travel to this single office every time they need a new passport, this office has branches (specific passport offices, or law enforcement agencies, depending on the country) all over the country. These offices (in many countries) do not issue the passport themselves, but simply validate the person's information and ask the main office to send them the passport, following which they give it to the person who requested it. Any person can walk into one of these offices and ask for a passport, which will be issued only after some controls (that are internationally decided) are passed. Any person holding a passport can walk into another country and can be recognized for what they are, even if it's the first time they arrive in that country. In addition, the central office of each country keeps a registry of each passport that has been issued, and in case the document is invalid before it's due, this is noted. The agent in the other country can directly ask the office of the country that has released the passport if the passport they are looking at is still valid or if it has been invalidated.

As you can imagine, this analogy is not perfect, but I think it is the best one. In this analogy, the person trusted by the other countries is the root CA, the office providing passports are the intermediate CA, the branches are the registration authority, the passport represents the digital certificate, and the barrier represents the end user. The registry in which every central office stores the invalidated passports can be compared to the **Certificate Revocation List** (**CRL**), where each CA puts the revoked certificates. As with a passport, a digital certificate can be revoked for multiple reasons. The most common are:

- The certificate expires.
- Some core information (such as the domain or IP) of the certificate changes and the certificate has not been updated.
- The certificate holder asks to revoke it. This often happens when the servers are compromised.
- A CA in its chain of trust has been compromised.

Signed certificates versus self-signed certificates

You can buy a signed certificate on several websites, and their price varies from $9.99/year to several thousand dollars per year. This is mainly because there are some certificates that allow you to cover multiple websites, have **Extended Validation** (**EV**) certificates, have different assurance on them, or have different brands. On the other hand, you can create your own CA and start creating your certificates free of charge. Does it make sense to buy a signed certificate?

Domain	Signed certificate	Self-signed certificate
Price	$9.99–$2000	Free
Issue time	1–14 days	Immediate
Browser compatibility	99.9%	Only browsers enabled by you or browser owner
Warranty	$5,000–$1.75 million	$0

As you can see, there are advantages and disadvantages on both sides. It really boils down to what you will do with this certificate. If you are willing to use it on a domain that will be Internet facing, I strongly suggest you to use a signed certificate. If you are going to use the certificate internally only, you can use your own CA and self-signed certificate. If you do so, remember to push your CA to all users' computers using a group policy or a custom package based on your environment.

Cipher security

As we have seen through this chapter, there are several algorithms for encryption, signing, and hashing, and each one has a different security level and has or could have known problems in the future. Therefore it is important to understand which algorithms are good to use and which are not, and obviously, how to communicate this to your software.

The majority of installations today rely on OpenSSL for all SSL/TLS encryption and decryption. OpenSSL can inform you about what algorithms you can use and their security status. To do so, you can execute it as follows:

```
$ openssl ciphers DEFAULT
ECDHE-RSA-AES256-GCM-SHA384:ECDHE-ECDSA-AES256-GCM-SHA384:ECDHE-RSA-
AES256-SHA384:ECDHE-ECDSA-AES256-SHA384:ECDHE-RSA-AES256-SHA:ECDHE-ECDSA-
AES256-SHA:DHE-DSS-AES256-GCM-SHA384:DHE-RSA-AES256-GCM-SHA384:DHE-RSA-
AES256-SHA256:DHE-DSS-AES256-SHA256:DHE-RSA-AES256-SHA:DHE-DSS-AES256-
SHA:DHE-RSA-CAMELLIA256-SHA:DHE-DSS-CAMELLIA256-SHA:ECDH-RSA-AES256-
GCM-SHA384:ECDH-ECDSA-AES256-GCM-SHA384:ECDH-RSA-AES256-SHA384:ECDH-
ECDSA-AES256-SHA384:ECDH-RSA-AES256-SHA:ECDH-ECDSA-AES256-SHA:AES256-
GCM-SHA384:AES256-SHA256:AES256-SHA:CAMELLIA256-SHA:PSK-AES256-CBC-
SHA:ECDHE-RSA-AES128-GCM-SHA256:ECDHE-ECDSA-AES128-GCM-SHA256:ECDHE-
RSA-AES128-SHA256:ECDHE-ECDSA-AES128-SHA256:ECDHE-RSA-AES128-SHA:ECDHE-
ECDSA-AES128-SHA:DHE-DSS-AES128-GCM-SHA256:DHE-RSA-AES128-GCM-SHA256:DHE-
RSA-AES128-SHA256:DHE-DSS-AES128-SHA256:DHE-RSA-AES128-SHA:DHE-DSS-
AES128-SHA:DHE-RSA-SEED-SHA:DHE-DSS-SEED-SHA:DHE-RSA-CAMELLIA128-SH-
A:DHE-DSS-CAMELLIA128-SHA:ECDH-RSA-AES128-GCM-SHA256:ECDH-ECDSA-AES128-
GCM-SHA256:ECDH-RSA-AES128-SHA256:ECDH-ECDSA-AES128-SHA256:ECDH-RSA-
AES128-SHA:ECDH-ECDSA-AES128-SHA:AES128-GCM-SHA256:AES128-SHA256:AES128-
SHA:SEED-SHA:CAMELLIA128-SHA:IDEA-CBC-SHA:PSK-AES128-CBC-SHA:KRB5-IDEA-
CBC-SHA:KRB5-IDEA-CBC-MD5:ECDHE-RSA-RC4-SHA:ECDHE-ECDSA-RC4-SHA:ECDH-RSA-
RC4-SHA:ECDH-ECDSA-RC4-SHA:RC4-SHA:RC4-MD5:PSK-RC4-SHA:KRB5-RC4-SHA:KRB5-
RC4-MD5:ECDHE-RSA-DES-CBC3-SHA:ECDHE-ECDSA-DES-CBC3-SHA:EDH-RSA-DES-
CBC3-SHA:EDH-DSS-DES-CBC3-SHA:ECDH-RSA-DES-CBC3-SHA:ECDH-ECDSA-DES-CBC3-
SHA:DES-CBC3-SHA:PSK-3DES-EDE-CBC-SHA:KRB5-DES-CBC3-SHA:KRB5-DES-CBC3-MD5
```

This is the list of algorithms that are enabled by default on my OpenSSL installation (version 1.0.1k on Fedora 21). If you have a different version or platform, you will probably have a different list. OpenSSL has multiple lists of algorithms; lists that contain unsafe algorithms are EXP (<=56 bits), LOW (>56 bits, <=64 bits) and MEDIUM (>64 bits, <=128 bits). To see which algorithms are parts of these groups, you can use the following commands:

```
$ openssl ciphers EXP
EXP-EDH-RSA-DES-CBC-SHA:EXP-EDH-DSS-DES-CBC-SHA:EXP-ADH-DES-CBC-SHA:EXP-
DES-CBC-SHA:EXP-RC2-CBC-MD5:EXP-RC2-CBC-MD5:EXP-KRB5-RC2-CBC-SHA:EXP-
KRB5-DES-CBC-SHA:EXP-KRB5-RC2-CBC-MD5:EXP-KRB5-DES-CBC-MD5:EXP-ADH-RC4-
MD5:EXP-RC4-MD5:EXP-RC4-MD5:EXP-KRB5-RC4-SHA:EXP-KRB5-RC4-MD5
$ openssl ciphers LOW
EDH-RSA-DES-CBC-SHA:EDH-DSS-DES-CBC-SHA:ADH-DES-CBC-SHA:DES-CBC-SHA:DES-
CBC-MD5:KRB5-DES-CBC-SHA:KRB5-DES-CBC-MD5
$ openssl ciphers MEDIUM
```

```
DHE-RSA-SEED-SHA:DHE-DSS-SEED-SHA:ADH-SEED-SHA:SEED-SHA:IDEA-CBC-
SHA:IDEA-CBC-MD5:RC2-CBC-MD5:KRB5-IDEA-CBC-SHA:KRB5-IDEA-CBC-MD5:ECDHE-
RSA-RC4-SHA:ECDHE-ECDSA-RC4-SHA:AECDH-RC4-SHA:ADH-RC4-MD5:ECDH-RSA-RC4-
SHA:ECDH-ECDSA-RC4-SHA:RC4-SHA:RC4-MD5:RC4-MD5:PSK-RC4-SHA:KRB5-RC4-
SHA:KRB5-RC4-MD5
```

As you will notice, toward the end of the DEFAULT ciphers list, there are few algorithms using the RC4 and/or the MD5 ciphers, which are known to be not very secure. In fact, you can find the same algorithms in the unsecure lists. Since we want to use only secure algorithms, we will use the following list of ciphers:

```
"HIGH:!RC4:!MD5:!aNULL:!eNULL:!EXP:!LOW:!MEDIUM"
```

This string will instruct OpenSSL to use all algorithms in the DEFAULT list and all algorithms in the HIGH list, with the exception of all algorithms using RC4, MD5, aNULL, and eNULL. Also, it will not use all algorithms listed in the EXP, LOW, and MEDIUM lists.

> It is critical to always keep your OpenSSL up to date. Algorithms that were believed to be safe until the day before could be discovered as broken overnight, so it's critical to always have those lists up to date. Also, always remember that OpenSSL is a software, and as a software, it could have its own bugs (like Heartbleed) that will need to be safely patched in minimal time to avoid any security problems.

Designing a redundant environment for your APIs

Before starting to talk about how to make a safe environment, I'd like to spend few words on how to make a redundant environment for your APIs. Since the APIs are a critical part of OpenStack, if they do not respond properly, the majority of operations OpenStack allows you to do will not be available.

There are many possibilities for designing a redundant service, but we will cover only the one that is by far the safest and the most redundant.

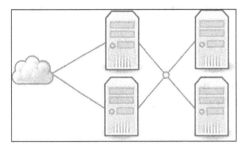

In this design, we have two load balancers that are both listed as A records in your DNSs. This will grant that even if one of the two dies somehow, the other will respond to all requests using the DNS round-robin; and while they are both up and running, they will split the traffic.

 Although the DNS round-robin will not grant you that your nodes will be hit by the same amount of traffic, it's a very inexpensive and reliable solution. It is for these reasons that I suggest this one.

Those frontend servers will use HAProxy to load balance and share the traffic between the API servers that are alive in that specific moment.

The API servers can use Apache httpd as well as many other web servers to serve the OpenStack API.

To make everything secure, both the connections (the one from the web to the frontend and the one from the frontend to the API server) will need to be encrypted. To do so, we will have to set up HAProxy to decrypt, process, and then re-encrypt the traffic. This allows us to use a public signed certificate and a private self-signed certificate, if we want to.

Although the configuration of HAProxy is not the focus of this book, I'm going to give you an example of a possible configuration for the situation pictured in the preceding image:

```
frontend tls
  bind *:443 ssl crt /etc/ssl/private/ ciphers
    HIGH:!RC4:!MD5:!aNULL:!eNULL:!EXP:!LOW:!MEDIUM no-sslv3
      default_backend openstack_api
```

```
backend openstack_api
  server api01 api01.internal:8447
  server api02 api02.internal:8447
```

HAProxy configurations tend to be pretty simple as soon as one familiarizes a little bit with it.

The first part (frontend) is where HAProxy looks to understand how to manage incoming connections, while the second part (backend) is where HAProxy looks to understand where to push requests.

So, looking at the fronted named `tls`, we give it a name, and we inform HAProxy that we want to manage all connections coming for the port 443 (HTTPS), that we will accept only a limited amount of ciphers, and that all those connections will have to be processed by the backend named `openstack_api`.

In the backend named `openstack_api`, we inform HAProxy to route all requests to the `api01.internal` and `api02.internal` nodes to the 8447 port (the API port). HAProxy will automatically load balance between the two and stop sending traffic to a node if this node fails.

Secure your OpenStack API with TLS

The first thing you have to do if you want to secure your APIs is to obtain a certificate that could either be signed or self-signed. Although the OpenStack API worker natively supports SSL/TLS, you'll need to use Apache httpd or nginx if you are willing to use external authentication systems such as Kerberos, SAML, or OpenID. Let's see how you can do so.

Apache HTTPd

In Apache httpd, to have a correctly set up system, we will need multiple `VirtualHost` to be precise, three.

The first one will respond on port 80 (HTTP) to redirect all users to port 443 (HTTPS). The following code is needed to force the usage of HTTPS:

```
<VirtualHost <ip address>:80>
  ServerName <site FQDN>
  RedirectPermanent / https://<site FQDN>/
</VirtualHost>
```

In this section, you have to enter your machine IP address and **Fully Qualified Domain Name (FQDN)**. For instance, in the local installation I have on my testing cluster, I will use the following statement:

```
<VirtualHost 192.168.122.15:80>
  ServerName api.test.local
  RedirectPermanent / https://api.test.local/
</VirtualHost>
```

> If you omit this first block, the most probable consequence is that users going to http://<site FQDN>/ will see an error instead of being redirected to the https://<site FQDN>/. In some situations, based on previous or default configurations of Apache httpd, different behaviors are possible, such as enabling navigation through APIs insecurely in HTTP.

The second part involves setting up the HTTPS VirtualHost and uses the following template:

```
<VirtualHost <ip address>:443>
  ServerName <site FQDN>
  SSLEngine On
  SSLProtocol +TLSv1 +TLSv1.1 +TLSv1.2
  SSLCipherSuite HIGH:!RC4:!MD5:!aNULL:!eNULL:!EXP:!LOW:!MEDIUM
  SSLCACertificateFile /path/<site FQDN>.crt
  SSLCertificateFile /path/<site FQDN>.crt
  SSLCertificateKeyFile /path/<site FQDN>.key
  WSGIScriptAlias / <WSGI script location>
  WSGIDaemonProcess horizon user=<user> group=<group> processes=3
    threads=10
  Alias /static <static files location>
  <Directory <WSGI dir>>
    # In Apache http server 2.4 and later:
    Require all granted
    # For http server 2.2 and earlier:
    # Order allow,deny
    # Allow from all
  </Directory>
</VirtualHost>
```

As you can see, there are several SSL options. Let's see what each one of them does:

- **SSLEngine On**: This enables the SSL for this `VirtualHost`.
- **SSLProtocol**: This instructs the SSL engine (usually OpenSSL) which versions of SSL and TLS to use. I usually use `+TLSv1 +TLSv1.1 +TLSv1.2`, which means that only TLS protocols are acceptable. This excludes SSLv2 and SSLv3, which have several security issues.
- **SSLCipherSuite**: This instructs the SSL engine (usually OpenSSL) which algorithms to use and which algorithms to avoid, as we have seen in the previous section.
- **SSLCACertificateFile**: This is the path to the CA certificate file.
- **SSLCertificateFile**: This is the path to the certificate file.
- **SSLCERTIFICATEKeyFile**: This is the path to the key file (private key) of your certificate.

The last section is needed to secure port 8447, where the API runs:

```
<VirtualHost <ip address>:8447>
  ServerName <site FQDN>
  SSLEngine On
  SSLProtocol +TLSv1 +TLSv1.1 +TLSv1.2
  SSLCipherSuite HIGH:!RC4:!MD5:!aNULL:!eNULL:!EXP:!LOW:!MEDIUM
  SSLCACertificateFile /path/<site FQDN>.crt
  SSLCertificateFile /path/<site FQDN>.crt
  SSLCertificateKeyFile /path/<site FQDN>.key
  WSGIScriptAlias / <WSGI script location>
  WSGIDaemonProcess osapi user=<user> group=<group> processes=3
  threads=10
  <Directory <WSGI dir>>
    # Or, in Apache http server 2.4 and later:
    Require all granted
    # For http server 2.2 and earlier:
    # Order allow,deny
    # Allow from all
  </Directory>
</VirtualHost>
```

As you can see, this third section is pretty similar to the previous one, with only a difference in the port.

Now you are ready to restart your Apache httpd, and you will find everything encrypted.

Nginx

In case you are using nginx instead of Apache httpd, this is an example of a config file to serve HTTPS:

```
server {
    listen : ssl;
    ssl_certificate /path/<site FQDN>.crt;
    ssl_certificate_key /path/<site FQDN>.key;
    ssl_protocols TLSv1.1 TLSv1.2;
    ssl_ciphers HIGH:!RC4:!MD5:!aNULL:!eNULL:!EXP:!LOW:!MEDIUM
    server_name <site FQDN>;
    keepalive_timeout 5;
    location / {
}
```

As you can see, even the names are very similar to the Apache httpd case, so it should be pretty straightforward.

Enforcing HTTPS for future connections

It is possible to ask the browser to require HTTPS connections every time it accesses that specific domain for a certain period. This could be a dangerous option, since if SSL breaks on the server side, that domain will be inaccessible until SSL is restored properly. On the other hand, it really increases security, because after the first HTTPS connection, you are granted that until the end of the set period, all communications will be fully encrypted. To do this, it is enough to send an HTTP Header like the following one in the response:

```
Strict-Transport-Security: max-age=86400; includeSubDomains
```

This example will make this option last for 24 hours. This could be a good value for testing purposes, while it would be a good idea to set it to longer periods (1 month or 1 year) in production environments.

Summary

In this chapter, we have seen what encryption, signing, and hashing are, and why they are relevant to you. We dove into how they work, to understand what possible threats are hidden in them. Then we moved to the PKI and certificate system to understand deeply how they work, and which vehicle of attacks is hidden there. In the last section, we saw how to secure OpenStack APIs.

In the next chapter, we will move on to securing the identification and authentication system of your OpenStack installation.

5
Securing the OpenStack Identification and Authentication System and Its Dashboard

Today we are used to be identified and authenticated to various types of systems. We start very early in the morning unlocking our phones (if it has a PIN or other kind of security). We do it continually on websites, smartphones, doors, and so on. We are so used to be identified and authenticated that a lot of times we do not focus enough on the importance and the security of this critical process. In this chapter, we will focus on each of those and how to secure them.

Identification versus authentication versus authorization

A lot of times, people use those words interchangeably, since they are performed at the same moment, but in reality, they are critically different concepts. We can define these three concepts as follows:

- **Identification**: This is an action in which the user (untrusted party) declares his identity
- **Authentication**: This is an action(s) to prove that the user is who he claims to be
- **Authorization**: This action(s) is required to determine which actions a specific user can perform

To bring this into the real world, let's take an easy example and analyze the various phases: a web login with the username and password.

Let's imagine you are logging into your OpenStack Dashboard. The username you put in the username field, is the identification part. In fact, you affirm to be yourself, and the system trusts you on this. However, to let you do anything, the system needs to authenticate you. To do so, it needs your password and will check whether the username and password match. After the system has authenticated you, it will look into the authorizations your account has in order to decide whether or not to show you the various links to resources. As you can see, these three items are different parts of the process, and it is important to understand each one of them to be able to manage a secure system.

Identification

Although the identification could seem to be useless because the system has to trust an untrusted party, it's critical to the security of the **Authentication**. In fact, the identification allows you to make the authentication problem a one-to-one problem, instead of a many-to-one problem, increasing its security by several orders of magnitude.

There are cases when it is acceptable to lower the security check a little bit, simplifying the identification phase to drastically reduce the amount of time needed for the process, making it less expensive. A typical example is badging to open a door. In this case, if you find a badge on the ground, you can enter without any problem since all the data is already present in the badge. On the other hand, if every time an employee's badge had to be identified by a security agent, you would see long lines of angry people waiting to be identified. In the badge example, the identification is usually done automatically, to make it quick enough to be cheap and effective.

Authentication

Authentication is one of the most attacked processes by malicious users, because it could be the weak link in the security chain.

There are instances when it is enough to be authenticated with a single method (**single factor authentication**), while there are other cases where more security is needed, so a **multiple factor authentication** is preferred.

The authentication can be performed in three different ways based on what you use to identify the person:

- **Something you know**: This is a way to identify a user using something like a PIN, a password, or a passphrase

- **Something you have**: This is a way to identify a user using something like a smart card or a badge
- **Something you are**: This is a way to identify a user using biometrical characteristics of the user.

Something you know

This is the most common way to authenticate a person.

In this method, there is a preshared secret between the parties that is revealed to ensure the identity of the other party.

As you can imagine this method can have multiple weak points:

- A secret can be revealed willingly or unwillingly to a third party
- If the preshared secret is heard/read by a third party, the third party can impersonate one of the parties
- Very often, the preshared secret is easy to remember
- Usually, people write down those secrets, in case they happen to forget them
- It is possible to replicate the knowledge without permission from the knowledge creator, so it is possible that multiple people know a preshared secret without the other party suspecting it

All in all, it's a low-to-medium level security method. There are some ways to be sure that the level of security is at least medium:

- Train people not to write down passwords, PIN, passphrases, codes, and so on
- Rotate passwords, but not too often (every 6 to 12 months)
- Prohibit the use of the password that has already been used in the history of that account
- Let people choose a password (this will help to prevent the need to write them down) enforcing some security rules or letting them choose between a set of passwords generated by the system
- Enforce basic security rules: a minimum of 11 characters for alphanumeric case sensitive passwords and 10 characters for passwords with all ASCII symbols
- Enforce at least a character for each character set (number, lowercase letters, uppercase letters, and special characters) available
- Prohibit the use of passwords present in the dictionary

- Prohibit the use of the company name, address, or any other company-related information
- Prohibit the use of personal information such as birthday, anniversary, spouse's birthday and name, or children's birthday and name

Something you have

As you can imagine, in this case, you need to physically have an item to be authenticated. This method of authentication is very common in offices using the badge.

This method has its downsides which are:

- A real object has to be created and delivered to each user
- As any other object, this item can be stolen

On the other side of the coin, both these downsides also have advantages, because of the fact that a real object has to be delivered to each user, which means that if the device gets stolen, it will travel at slow speed and will be possible to block it before it's used. Also, a lot of times, people put their badges in their wallet and if their wallet gets stolen, chances are the thieves do not know what to do with the badge and will dump it. Also, people will soon know that their security device has been stolen, so they will be able to contact the IT department to get it locked.

For those reasons, this kind of authentication can be very effective.

Something you are

Today passwords and badges are becoming old fashioned, according to any consumer electronics company. Even if all the behavioral (also known as **behaviometrics**) characteristics fall into this category, today there is a huge push for biometrics. I think this is, at least, partially caused by Hollywood films that years ago started ago to portray super-secure systems that are opened with biometric information.

The most common biometric identifiers are:

- DNA
- Face recognition
- Fingerprint
- Hand geometry
- Palm print
- Palm veins

- Iris recognition
- Retina recognition

The most common behavioral characteristics are:

- Typing rhythm
- Gait
- Voice
- Hand-written signature

Some of these technological advances have just hit the mass market and many of those are yet to be seen in the mass market, so it's hard to compare them to the other two factors, which have been used intensively for decades. A few things that need to be considered are:

- These characteristics are hard (for behavioral) or impossible (for biometric) to change, so if they are compromised, it's difficult to re-set everything back to normal.

- These characteristics are absolutely not secrets. It's easy to get DNA from a person, since it is easy to get a hair (a complete one) or a fingerprint (that is, from a cup or other objects a person touches) or iris images from pictures posted on social networks, and so on.

- Unlike the other two options where the matches are always right (if you have inserted the right password, it will match, and if you have inserted the wrong password the system will deny your authentication; and the same applies for security tokens) it's possible that your face does not match (perhaps you forgot to trim your beard) or another similar face could be matched.

For these reasons, I would not consider this a secure authentication method, at least if used alone. Today, we see more and more mobile devices requiring some kind of biometric identifiers to unlock the phone or similar features. I think this is a feasible usage of those technologies since the users are often too lazy to put a PIN code on their phone, while they are happy to swipe their fingerprint on the fingerprint reader. In this case, even if it is not the safest solution, it is much safer than the current one and is acceptable to the users.

The multifactor authentication

As you have probably noticed, all the options we have discussed cannot be considered alone because each one of them has their own weaknesses. The good thing is that each option has different kinds of weaknesses, so if they are combined they can create a very secure system.

Currently, the most widespread multifactor authentication is the one that combines the **knowledge factor** and the **ownership factor**. The examples of those implementations are everywhere around us. Many banks provide their customers with an OTP (one time password) generator that is needed for every online operation. When an OTP (that is a physical object) is needed together with a password (that is known as a string), you have an example of a two-factor authentication.

Authorization

The authorization is the third and last step of the process. The goal of authorization is to be sure that the given user has clearance to do what he is asking to do.

It is important that the three steps of the chain—identification, authentication, and authorization—are performed correctly, because if one of them fails, the whole security chain will fail.

There are multiple ways to grant privileges to a user, based on the access control model the system uses. The main access control models are:

- **Mandatory Access Control (MAC)**
- **Discretionary Access Control (DAC)**
- **Role-based Access Control (RBAC)**
- **Lattice-based Access Control (LBAC)**

Mandatory Access Control

The MAC paradigm is very good if you don't trust your users, since you are only allowed to let new people. The downside is that it's very hard to keep up with all the permissions if your company is growing because very often the workload on the security administrators increases more than the linear increase of the people and projects your company manages.

 In the MAC paradigm, the Security Administrator allows people to access the determined resources and no one else can change it.

A good example of MAC is SELinux, a MAC architecture for Linux Kernel developed by NSA.

Discretionary Access Control

The DAC paradigm is very good if you are in a pretty big company where people are aware of the consequences of opening a resource to more people. Each team manager will manage the access of its team granting it to newcomers and deactivating people that move out of the team. The risk is that people who don't care enough about security or are not paying enough attention, will leave their documents available to more people than needed violating the confidentiality of it.

[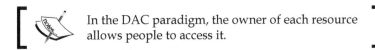 In the DAC paradigm, the owner of each resource allows people to access it.]

A good example of DAC is the UNIX user permissions systems.

Role-based Access Control

The RBAC can use both DAC and MAC paradigms, and works on top of them. While the DAC and MAC regulate who is able to grant permissions, the RBAC regulates how precisely they will be given.

The RBAC approach can help in reducing the amount of work needed to manage the permissions, as in the example we will see next.

This company has a huge Information System that manages pretty much everything that happens in the company, including all user permissions. When they employ a new person, let's say in accounting, they simply need to tell the system that particular person is now an employee, is working in the accounting department, and has a certain badge ID. The system will set up an account for this person with all the privileges that he needs and to grant him badge access to certain areas of the building, where the accountants are supposed to have access. This is also possible the other way round: when someone leaves, the system can block all his accounts and clearance, or when someone changes department his permissions will match the new department's privileges or both the departments' privileges, if he is working in both of them.

RBAC systems are very common and most companies that employ over a few hundred people use such systems.

Lattice-based Access Control

The LBAC approach, like the RBAC, is useful to reduce the amount of permissions that need to be managed since the amount of work grows strictly linearly with the linear increase of people and resources. The downside of this approach, and the reason why I don't really like it is that the people in the highest positions in the company have full access to all resources, which does not make sense, usually.

In the LBAC, often known as Label-based Access Control or Rule-based Access Control, each resource or object has a security level, and each person has a security level. If the security level of the person is equal to or greater than the security level of the resource or object he is wishing to use, they will be able to use it.

Session management

After the identification, authentication, and authorization process, a session is created so that the user can interact with the system for a certain amount of time without having to pass these three steps each time. Tokens are used to identify those sessions. By default, in OpenStack, from the Icehouse release, all sessions expire after 1 hour, while previous releases used 24 hours as the session lifespan. It may make sense to reduce this time even more, since if an malicious user can take control of a machine within a valid session, he will be able to act as if he is the owner of the session. Decreasing the length of sessions means reducing the window in which an attacker can steal a session.

There are some jobs such as transferring a disk image to the hypervisor for local caching that might require long time. If your session lifespan is shorter than the time those jobs need, they will probably fail.

Federated identity

Majority of the companies today have multiple services, each one requiring an authentication. For years, companies have chosen to have multiple databases of users, one for each service. Although this worked for a long time, since the majority of companies only had one or two services, this is not working any more, since today, a lot of companies have tens of services. This redundant approach, apart from being very confusing for the users, exposes a lot of potential security problems.

In fact, it's easier for a malicious person to gain an account on a system in this case, because he will have multiple people to trick. Also, since when a new person is recruited, many accounts will need to be created. It is likely that fewer checks will be done for each account creation, leaving the system less secure.

Today, it is possible to create **Federated identity**, which are accounts provided by an **Identity Provider** (**IdP**) to one or many **Service Provider** (**SP**). Using this approach, you'll simply have to create an Identity Provider, create all accounts on it and configure all your services to trust the identity validation to the Identity Provider instead of doing it internally in the code. Doing so every time a new person is recruited will be enough to create a single account on the Identity Provider and all services will automatically recognize the new employee. Also, when a person leaves the company, it will be enough to lock a single account on the Identity Provider to lock all services to this person.

An example of how a login on a system in a federated identity environment is can be seen in the following diagram:

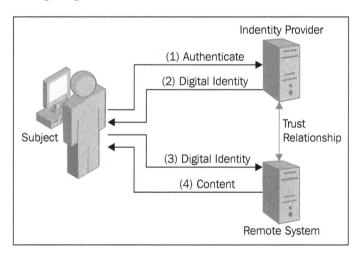

Configuring OpenStack Keystone to use Apache HTTPd

To allow OpenStack to use an external Identity Provider or to become an Identity Provider itself, the first thing to to is enable Keystone to use HTTPd.

Firstly, install `httpd`, `mod_nss`, `mod_wsgi`, and `python-paste-deploy`. To do so under `RedHat/CentOS 6 and 7`, run the following command:

```
yum install httpd mod_nss mod_wsgi python-paste-deploy
```

For other distributions, check the specific documentation of your distribution since some package names might be different.

Apache HTTPd configuration

Let's start configuring Apache HTTPd. You need to run Apache HTTPd on port 443 instead of port 8443 that is set by default. We have to change `/etc/httpd/conf.d/nss.conf` in two places. First of all, you need to find the following string around line 10:

```
Listen 8443
```

Then you need to substitute it with the following:

```
Listen 443
```

The other necessary change to this file is done a few lines later, where the following code appears:

```
<virtualhost _default_:8443="">
```

It should be substituted with the following:

```
<virtualhost _default_:443="">
```

We now need to copy the keystone configuration file to `/etc/httpd/conf.d/`. In `RedHat/CentOS`, it is not provided with the packages, so we will download it from the OpenStack GitHub repository:

```
cd /etc/httpd/conf.d/
wget
https://raw.githubusercontent.com/openstack/keystone/stable/juno/http
d/wsgi-keystone.conf
```

Making Keystone available to Apache HTTPd

To make Keystone available for Apache HTTPd, we need to create links to the keystone folder at `wsgi in the /var/www/cgi-bin/keystone`:

```
mkdir /var/www/cgi-bin/keystone
ln /usr/share/keystone/keystone.wsgi /var/www/cgi-bin/keystone/main
ln /usr/share/keystone/keystone.wsgi /var/www/cgi-bin/keystone/admin
```

Configuring iptables

In case you are using iptables, add the rule that will open port 443 to `/etc/sysconfig/iptables` or something equivalent:

```
-A INPUT -m state --state NEW -m tcp -p tcp --dport 443 -j ACCEPT
```

Remember that you need to put this rule before the **catch-all rule** that is usually placed in the last line of that file.

Configuring firewalld

Today, all distributions are moving towards systemd. If you are running one of those systems, such as CentOS/RHEL 7, chances are you have firewalld running. In this case, you'll need to configure it instead of iptables:

```
firewall-cmd --permanent --zone=internal --add-port=443/tcp
```

SELinux

If you have SELinux enabled on the machine, and you should since this will increase a lot the security of your system, you'll need a new policy to allow OpenStack Keystone to run properly. To do so, you'll need to create a SELinux policy package.

Let's start by creating the folder where we will be working:

```
mkdir /root/keystonewsgi
cd /root/keystonewsgi
```

Then we need to create the `keystonewsgi.te` file with the following content to instruct SELinux to accept attempts of Apache HTTPd to operate on files and folders tagged with the keystone label:

```
policy_module(keystonewsgi, 1.0.0)

require {
  type httpd_t;
  type keystone_var_lib_t;
}

allow httpd_t keystone_var_lib_t:dir { search getattr };
allow httpd_t keystone_var_lib_t:file { read write getattr open
  setattr };
```

After this, your SELinux Policy Package is almost ready to be compiled. To be ready, you'll need to link the default SELinux `Makefile`:

```
ln -s /usr/share/selinux/devel/Makefile.
```

Now, you are ready to build the package, so you can run the `make` command:

```
make
```

And as soon as the compilation ends, you can install your SELinux Policy Package:

```
semodule -i keystonewsgi.pp
```

Setting up shared tokens

Since Apache HTTPd can run multiple threads at the same time, you cannot keep the session's tokens in memory, because they would not be available to the thread that is responding to a request. To allow Apache HTTPd threads to share the session's tokens, you'll need to edit `/etc/keystone/keystone.conf`.

If you plan to use SQL:

```
[token]
driver = keystone.token.backends.sql.Token
```

If you plan to use `memcache`:

```
[token]
driver = keystone.token.backends.memcache.Token
```

 Remember that a SQL server or a `memcache` server has to be present and to be configured to work properly.

Setting up the startup properly

Since you already have the Openstack-Keystone service running, you'll need to stop it and prevent it from starting again.

If you are on CentOS/RHEL 6, you'll need to run the following:

```
service openstack-keystone stop
chkconfig openstack-keystone off
```

If you are on CentOS/RHEL 7, you'll need to run the following:

```
systemctl stop openstack-keystone
systemctl disable openstack-keystone
```

On the other hand, you'll need Apache HTTPd to be running and to be started at machine startup. Since Apache HTTPd could be already running, to be sure that all your changes have been applied, you'll need to stop it beforehand.

If you are on CentOS/RHEL 6, you'll need to run the following:

```
service httpd restart
chkconfig httpd on
```

If you are on CentOS/RHEL 7, you'll need to run the following:

```
systemctl restart httpd
systemctl enable httpd
```

Setting up Keystone as a Identity Provider

If you want to set up Keystone to use an external Identity Provider, you'll need to set up a few more parts.

 To set up Keystone to connect to another Identity Provider, you need to have already configured OpenStack Keystone to use Apache HTTPd.

The first thing to do is install Shibboleth as follows:

```
yum install shibboleth
```

Configuring Apache HTTPd

To make Shibboleth work properly, we need to change /etc/httpd/conf.d/wsgi-keystone.conf by adding the following lines:

```
WSGIScriptAliasMatch ^(/v3/OS-
FEDERATION/identity_providers/.*?/protocols/.*?/auth)$
/var/www/keystone/main/$1


<Location /Shibboleth.sso>
  SetHandler shib
```

```
</Location>

<LocationMatch /v3/OS-
FEDERATION/identity_providers/.*?/protocols/saml2/auth>
  ShibRequestSetting requireSession 1
  AuthType shibboleth
  ShibRequireAll On
  ShibRequireSession On
  ShibExportAssertion Off
  Require valid-user
</LocationMatch>
```

The first line adds a new Alias for the `keystone.wsgi` file.

Both the locations are needed by Shibboleth to work properly.

 In the `LocationMatch` block, we have a Regular Expression with the protocol `saml2` hardcoded into it. In some cases, you might use a different protocol. If this is the case, fix the regex appropriately. Never use the wildcard (*) for that field, because this could create a security problem on your system.

Restart Apache HTTPd to apply the changes.

If you are on CentOS/RHEL 6, run the following:

```
service httpd restart
```

If you are on CentOS/RHEL 7, run the following:

```
systemctl restart httpd
```

Configuring Shibboleth

To make Shibboleth work properly, a couple of steps are required.

First of all, we need to create a certificate. Doing so is important to choose the length of the certificate, as follows:

```
shib-keygen -y NUMBER_OF_YEARS
```

After this, you'll need to copy the file that has just been created at `/etc/shibboleth/sp-key.pem` to your Identity Provider.

Be sure that in `/etc/shibboleth/shibboleth2.xml` the environment variable `REMOTE_USER` is not set; otherwise, local users will not be able to log in.

Restart Shibboleth as follows to apply the changes:

```
service shibd restart
```

To make Shibboleth work properly, we need to ensure that, after every reboot, it will be executed automatically. To do so, run the following code:

```
chkconfig shibd on
```

Configuring OpenStack Keystone

To make Keystone work in a Federated environment, add the following code to `/etc/keystone/keystone.conf`:

```
[federation]
driver = keystone.contrib.federation.backends.sql.Federation


[auth]
methods = external,password,token,saml2
saml2 = keystone.auth.plugins.saml2.Saml2
```

Add the following two lines to `/etc/keystone/keystone-paste.ini`:

```
[pipeline:api_v3]
pipeline = access_log sizelimit url_normalize token_auth
admin_token_auth xml_body json_body ec2_extension s3_extension
federation_extension service_v3
```

Refresh the Keystone database with:

```
keystone-manage db_sync --extension federation
```

Summary

In this chapter, we have seen what identification, authentication, and authorization are and what their weak points could be. After this, we moved to OpenStack Keystone and looked at how to enable Apache HTTPd with SSL, and how to enable the federation.

In the next chapter, we will look at the storage systems and their security aspects.

Securing OpenStack Storage

When the word **storage** is mentioned in clusters and other complete architectures, we can refer to three possible kinds:

- Object storage
- Block storage
- File storage

In this chapter, we will focus on how OpenStack provides storage. Our focus, as usual, will be more on the security part than on others, such as performance.

OpenStack provides two different storage services, **Cinder** and **Swift**. Both these components, like the majority of OpenStack components, don't act directly but use backends.

Different storage types

As we have seen, three major paradigms in storage define the kind of storage we are dealing with. Each one has its advantages and disadvantages. Let's look at each one of them to understand what you need.

Object storage

Object storage manages files as objects and allows your applications to manage files, not caring about where they stay and how big they are. I think the best explanation of object storage was given to me by a senior system administrator a few years ago:

Object storage is like valet parking. You arrive with your car, give it to the valet, and in exchange, you receive a ticket. When you need your car again, you hand back the ticket and the valet provides you with your car in exchange. As it often happens with metaphors, it doesn't fit perfectly because, for instance, in object storage you can get the same object multiple times, while with cars you can only get it once, but I think this comparison is a very good one. In fact, the similarities are several:

- Both systems are directly accessible; in fact, Object Systems are usually accessible via HTTP and car parking is usually easily accessible from the roads.
- In both systems, you don't care where your belongings (object in the object storage, car in the parking) will end up being.
- In both systems, you have something that identifies your belongings (ID for object storage, ticket for parking).
- Both systems allow some security for belongings (authentication system for object storage and car keys for the parking).

Object storage has huge advantages over the other kinds of storage due to the abstraction and the self-management it offers. It can increase its size if you provide it with more hard drives. It can also remove broken drives from its pool without losing the data that was kept on those drives. Other advantages that object storage offers are connected to its architecture, which allows us to save billions of files and total volumes of exabytes, without the need for defragmentation or other processes that common storage systems demand.

As with all technology, object storage has its drawbacks as well. Object storage systems are optimized for fast reading, not for fast writing, so if your application writes a lot of data, object storage will not be a good option for you.

In OpenStack, the Swift component provides object storage capabilities.

Block storage

You can think of block storage as traditional hard disks, since this is exactly how the machines will see it. Due to this, it's very easy to move from traditional hard disks to block storage. Usually, block storage is exported using one of the following protocols:

- **Fibre Channel (FC)**
- **Fibre Channel over Ethernet (FCoE)**
- **Internet Small Computer System Interface (iSCSI)**

Fibre channel connections allow higher speeds and lower latencies but require fibre channel ports and switches.

The FCoE and the iSCSI protocols are limited by the Ethernet protocol, which has quite high latency (compared to the FC protocol). By default, iSCSI is used by OpenStack since this allows running on commodity hardware without having to install fiber channel networks.

The main disadvantage of block storage is the absence of linear scalability. To make a poorly performing block device perform better, you cannot simply add more disks to it (although this does work on certain kind of speed problems). The best way to improve its performance is to put higher performance drives (that is, HDDs with higher throughput or SSD) or to use a higher performing RAID underneath it.

Also, block storages used to be limited in terms of maximum disk size and maximum file size depending on the filesystem, as shown in the following table:

Filesystem	Max device size	Max file size
EXT3	32 TiB	2 TiB
EXT4	1 EiB	16 TiB
FAT32	2 TiB	2 GiB
XFS	16 EiB	8 EiB -1
ZFS	252 ZiB	16 EiB

As you can see, the modern filesystems are allowing bigger devices and bigger file sizes, but they still tend to slow down as they get fuller.

In OpenStack, the Cinder component provides block storage capabilities.

File storage

File storage is somehow in between the two. In fact, file storage presents to the operative system a filesystem where the operative system, its applications, and its users can read and write as if it was a local file system. The difference between block storage and file storage is that block storage presents itself to the operative system as a bare disk, while the file storage presents itself as a filesystem. Even if this difference can seem to be irrelevant, it's more relevant and its implications are huge.

Block storages, being disks, can be given to only a single machine in read/write mode. These are different from physical disks, which can be assigned to multiple machines as read-only drives. On the other hand, file storage is managed by the server machine, and the client machine can only access the disk by speaking through the server machine. This allows the server to talk to multiple machines at the same time (thus, multiple machines can read and write on the filesystem), and simultaneously keep the filesystem consistent and healthy.

File storage is not new. SUN, in 1984, published a filesystem that did something very similar: the **Network File System** (**NFS**), which is still used today in various environments. Another similar filesystem that is commonly used is **Server Message Block** (**SMB**), also known as **Common Internet File System** (**CIFS**).

OpenStack does not offer an official component that completely handles these kinds of storage yet. However, in the Kilo release, the **Manila** component will probably be added, which will be able to handle NFS and SMB servers. Also, two important backends of OpenStack (**Ceph** and **GlusterFS**) support this kind of storage by default.

Comparison between storage solutions

Usually, more than a single storage solution is configured in each cluster, since usually the applications that run in the cluster have reasons to use more than a single solution. Let's compile the differences between the various solutions in the following table:

Feature	Block storage	File storage	Object storage
Scalability	Less than linear	Less than linear	Linear
Ways to access the data	iSCSI, FC, FCoE	NFS, SMB, Proprietary	HTTP(S), Proprietary
Number of concurrent users	1	Limited	Unlimited
Security policy level	Block	Filesystem	File
Versioning	Absent	Absent	Usually present

These are not the only differences between these types of storage. The important differences between them are in the security domain.

Security

First, for all the aforementioned types of storage, we must remember that data will move between different physical nodes (indicatively from storage nodes to computing nodes). Though pretty obvious, this can have a huge impact on security, since in the traditional model where in the same chassis you had the data and the computing power to process them, there was pretty much no way to spoof the connection between the hard drive and the CPU. In the model in which storage and computing power are in different nodes, data will pass through your infrastructure. For this reason, the majority of backends support encryption, but this could cause delay or increase the machine's load significantly. On the other side of the coin, those systems usually disperse data in multiple machines, so it's even harder to find all data that is logically connected.

Since each storage system works differently and with different assumptions, in my experience is more relevant for security the specific storage system more than it' kind (block storage, file storage, or object storage), and even more so today since many of them implement more than one storage type.

Backends

Backends are critical since these software are the real holders of your data. This means that if the backend you are using ends up having a major security flaw, chances are, you'll be afflicted. The main backends are as follows:

Backend	Block storage	File storage	Object storage
Ceph	Yes	Yes	Yes
GlusterFS	Yes	Yes	Yes
LVM	Yes	No	No
NFS	Yes	Yes	No
Sheepdog	Yes	No	Yes
Swift	No	No	Yes
ZFS	Yes	No	No

As you can see, several options can be used as backends. Let's look at each one of them more specifically.

Ceph

Ceph was created by Sage Weil (co-founder of DreamHost) in a doctoral dissertation in 2007. After completing his doctorate, he continued to work on Ceph, and few years later (2011), he approached Inktank Storage to provide commercial support for Ceph. In April 2014, Red Hat acquired Inktank Storage for $175 million.

Ceph is composed of an object store called **Reliable, Autonomous, Distributed Object Store (RADOS)**, on which multiple components rely. Two components rely directly on RADOS:

- **librados**: This refers to a set of libraries to interact in an easy way with RADOS in many languages, including C, C++, Java, Python, Ruby, and PHP.

- **CephFS**: This refers to a distributed filesystem that is POSIX-compliant and accessible through an official Linux Kernel module (in the mainstream since Linux 2.6.34) and FUSE. This component provides file storage capability.

Two more components have been built upon librados:

- **RADOS Gateway (RADOSGW)**: This is a REST gateway that provides the object storage capability and is compatible with the S3 and Swift API.

- **RADOS Block Device (RBD)**: This is the provider of block storage capability that has a Linux Kernel client (since Linux 2.6.34), which allows any Linux machine with a modern kernel or anything that is virtualized upon QEMU/KVM to use the block storages properly. To summarize, this is the architecture of Ceph:

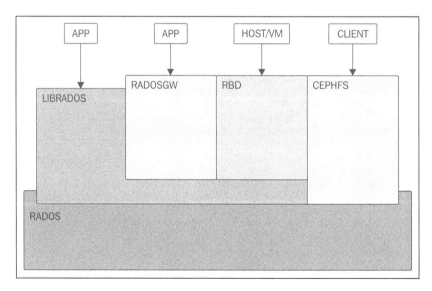

The biggest known installation of Ceph is the **DreamObject** Cloud Store by DreamHost, which is over 3 PB.

GlusterFS

GlusterFS was developed by **Gluster Inc.**, and since 2005, it has been made open source. In fact, the name Gluster arrives from the contraction of the words *GNU* and *cluster*. In 2011, Red Hat bought Gluster Inc. and since then has been the main developer of Gluster.

GlusterFS is composed of a server (glusterfsd) that runs on the storage nodes and a client (glusterfs) that run on the head nodes. The communication between servers and clients uses a custom protocol that runs over TCP/IP, InfiniBand, or **Sockets Direct Protocol (SDP)**. The head nodes will then expose the kind of storage needed using the built-in translator.

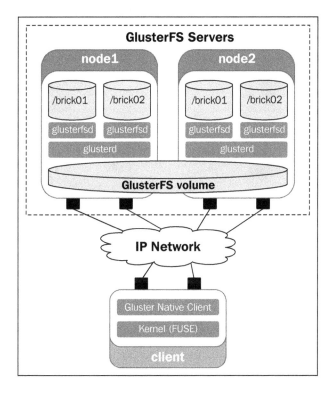

The server part of GlusterFS is kept simple by design to minimize possible problems, while the client part provides the majority of features. To grant maximum flexibility, clients don't need to communicate with each other and are stateless. Also, GlusterFS does not rely on metadata storage but uses an elastic hashing algorithm.

GlusterFS is capable of exposing block storage, object storage, and file storage. It can export object storage in multiple formats including the OpenStack Swift format. It can also export file storage in multiple formats, including SMB and NFS.

The biggest known installation of GlusterFS is in the Brightcove infrastructure with over 1 PB installed.

The Logical Volume Manager

The **Logical Volume Manager** (**LVM**) was written in 1998 by Heinz Mauelshagen, inspired by HP-UX's volume manager. Today, all Linux distributions are LVM-aware and a majority of them will use it in their default installation.

LVM works on three levels: the **Physical Volume** (**PV**), which refers to the physical drives on your machine; the **Volume Group** (**VG**), which are groups of PVs; and the **Logical Volume** (**LV**), which refers to the single partitions that your operative system will handle.

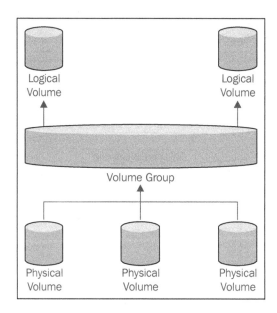

This allows LVM to perform many magical operations, such as moving a live partition from a disk to another or live resizing, as well as many other very handy operations.

Since it's a very widespread technology and probably the majority of your machines use LVM in one way or another, I'd like to bring up an example of simple typos that can kill your machine.

A few years ago, one of my clients had a MySQL database growing beyond expectations, so a bigger disk become necessary. This operation is safe enough to be executed at system live during business hours, so there was a MySQL running on that partition reading and writing at full speed. A senior administrator created a new LUN on the SAN and then moved it to the machine to add the new LUN to the VG. The next operation was to extend the LV by 300 GB. The right command to do so would be:

```
lvextend -L+300G /dev/vg_database/lv_database
```

But in this command, even a small error can be catastrophic if you make the following error:

```
lvextend -L300G /dev/vg_database/lv_database
```

In this case, the partition will not be increased by 300 GB, but its size will be set to 300 GB. When you have a 700 GB partition, close to becoming completely full, and it is suddenly resized to 300 GB, the filesystem will be corrupted. MySQL will fail and you'll face a huge amount of data loss, meaning that you'll spend the next few days restoring data (hopefully you'll have backups and a way to recreate the data from last backup).

 Due to its ancient design, LVM performs very dangerous operations without confirmation, so always double-check your commands.

The Network File System

The **Network File System (NFS)** was developed by SUN Microsystem in 1984. In 2001, NFSv4 was released; it was the first version maintained by the **Internet Engineering Task Force (IETF)** after SUN handed over the NFS protocol development.

The NFS protocol works in a server-client mode in which the clients do not have direct access to the disk but have to ask the server to read (or write) a file or folder on their behalf.

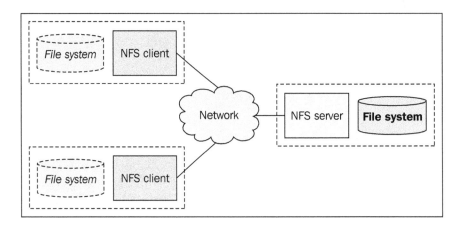

Sheepdog

Sheepdog was created in 2009 by the Nippon Telegraph and Telephone Corporation, and it provides both object storage and block storage.

The block storage API is designed to allow direct attachment of Sheepdog block storage to Linux SCSI Target as well as many other formats. The object storage API is designed to be compatible with both the Amazon Web Services S3 API and OpenStack Swift API.

The Nippon Telegraph and Telephone Corporation have shown some benchmarks that they executed, which show that in many situations, Sheepdog performs sensibly better than other, more common systems, such as Ceph.

No big production installations of Sheepdog are known to exist, probably because this project is very young compared to its counterparts.

Swift

Swift is one of the two components in the first OpenStack release. It was created in 2009 by **Rackspace** as a replacement for the Cloud Files product they had earlier. Today, **SwiftStack** is the company that is continuing the development of Swift.

Swift is the only one in this list that is not an external software used as a backend for OpenStack. Swift is usable only through OpenStack or SwiftStack, which is based on OpenStack. Since it is an integral part of OpenStack, it offers the best compatibility with OpenStack, and all features are nicely manageable directly from OpenStack itself. The downside is that there are no major installations outside the OpenStack world.

What differentiates Swift from the majority of the other solutions is that it is an eventually consistent type of object storage; so, the consistency has been sacrificed to obtain better performance and scalability.

Swift has huge installations around the world, since it's used in a majority of OpenStack clouds. Examples include the Rackspace cloud, the HP cloud, and Marcado Libre, which has deployed a 1.2 PB Swift system.

Z File System (ZFS)

The development of ZFS began in 2001 at the Sun Corporation, but it became public only in 2004. In 2005, it became a part of Solaris, and in the same year, its code base was released. Due to some licensing issues, ZFS was never brought into the Linux Kernel, even if implementations of ZFS for Linux are available (mainly a native one and a FUSE-based one). Today, the best options for ZFS are Solaris and the various BSD systems that ship it.

From a technical point of view, ZFS is an amazing filesystem promising to be able to handle up to 256 ZB (1 ZB is 1024 EB) per volume. From a practical point of view, I see the operating system limitation as too limiting to use it, unless you are already planning to use Solaris or BSD for your cluster.

Security

The first thing to do if you want to obtain safer storage is to keep it in a different VLAN from the rest of the traffic. This will slow down any kind of attack to your storage infrastructure; in fact, it will not be possible for the computing nodes to tap into the storage network.

 Multiple storage systems do not encrypt data between storage nodes, so a completely dedicated (V)LAN is needed for security reasons.

Another thing you should do to improve the security of your system is to run all storage processes with limited root (not root).

Securing OpenStack Swift

Since Swift is the single most-used storage for OpenStack and chances are you'll deploy it too, let's dive into how to secure OpenStack Swift. Also, similar suggestions can be used for the majority of other backends.

A good design is necessary for storage security. A typical design for Swift is as follows:

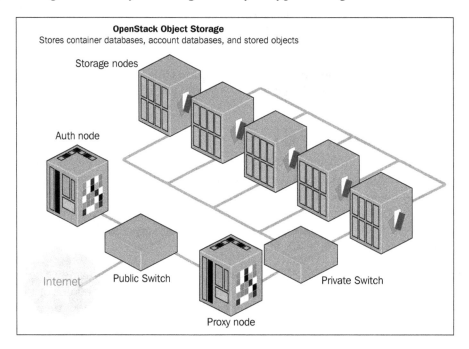

Hiding information

If you have followed the suggestion given in the preceding section on *Security*, you should be running OpenStack Swift as a non-root user. Let's suppose you are running Swift using the user **swift** in the group called **swift** for the sake of the example.

Since Swift (as well as the 99.99 percent of programs in Linux) does not need to modify its own config file, you can perform the following operations to ensure that the Swift user will be able to read its configurations but will not be able to change them.

To do so, you can assign to the /etc/swift folder (and all subfolders and files) the user root (as it should already be) and group swift.

```
chown -R root:swift /etc/swift/*
```

At this point, we can assign the permission 640 to all files and 750 to all folders.

```
find /etc/swift/ -type f -exec chmod 640 {} \;
find /etc/swift/ -type d -exec chmod 750 {} \;
```

 Remember that folders have to have the executable bit to allow you to look up the files in them.

Securing ports

Swift, like many other storage systems, uses a number of services to sync between the various storage nodes. The clients do not need authentication since Swift assumes that it's working on a trusted network.

Swift uses the following services:

- Account service 6002/TCP
- Container service 6001/TCP
- Object service 6000/TCP
- Rsync 873/TCP

In case you are using Ssync instead of Rsync, the port 6000/TCP will be used for this to maintain durability.

You should firewall these ports from all IPs excluding the nodes. Depending on your networking hardware, you will need to perform different operations to do so.

If you are implementing the suggested architecture, you can obtain this by making some very strict rules on the firewall to allow traffic to pass only on the HTTPS port, closing all the other ports.

To do so, you will need to run the following commands:

```
iptables -A INPUT -p tcp -m tcp -m multiport --dports 443 -j
ACCEPT
iptables -A INPUT -m conntrack -j ACCEPT   --ctstate
RELATED,ESTABLISHED
iptables -A INPUT -m state --state ESTABLISHED,RELATED -j ACCEPT
iptables -A INPUT -j DROP
iptables -A OUTPUT -m state --state ESTABLISHED,RELATED -j ACCEPT
iptables -A OUTPUT -j DROP
iptables -A FORWARD -m state --state ESTABLISHED,RELATED -j ACCEPT
iptables -A FORWARD -j DROP
```

This will allow only traffic on port 443 to enter your proxy machine. If you are connected in **Secure Shell (SSH)** to the machine and you run those commands, your connection will be dropped and you will not be able to access the machine using SSH. Please remember to open all other ports that you need (IE: 22 for SSH).

Summary

In this chapter, we saw which options you could choose to create your OpenStack Storage, along with some aspects that are not completely technical but can influence your decision. After this, we moved on to see how to secure OpenStack Swift, one of the most commonly deployed Storage systems of OpenStack.

In the next chapter, we will look at computing from the security point of view with respect to the different hypervisors and their meaning in terms of security.

7
Securing the Hypervisor

Today, wherever you look at IT, the main word that anyone says is **virtualization**. We are moving towards a virtualization of storage, networking, and even computing.

Initially, the word virtualization was used only for computing, in the sense of creating some kind of virtual resource to be used instead of the actual (physical) one. There are multiple software solutions that allow you to use virtualization.

Various types of virtualization

The virtualization of computing resources is possible thanks to a specific software called hypervisor. It's possible to classify hypervisors in categories based on the amount of hardware that is virtualized and the number of modifications the guest system requires.

Usually, virtualizations are divided into three categories based on how much and what is virtualized:

- Full virtualization
- Paravirtualization
- Partial virtualization

Full virtualization

In a fully virtualized environment, each component that the virtual machine provides to the operative system is virtualized, so a standard operative system can be run without any modification. Usually, the hypervisor simulates a very specific hardware, for instance, QEMU — simulating an x86 machine will always provide a (virtual) Realtek 8139C+ PCI as the network adapter. This makes the guest operative system unaware of the fact that it is not running on real hardware.

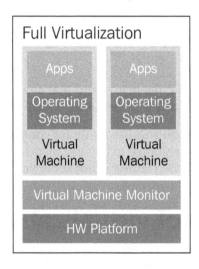

On the other side of the coin, having multiple levels of redundant abstraction, full virtualization will waste more resources than any other type of virtualization. Historically, this meant a big decrease in performance, but today, this is less true thanks to the advancement of hardware-aid virtualization.

In terms of security, full virtualization is safer, since nothing is shared between virtual machines; so if one is compromised, it is not possible to compromise anything else unless a **hypervisor breakout** occurs.

Several hypervisors use full virtualization, such as QEMU, VirtualBox, VMware ESXi, and many others.

Paravirtualization

In paravirtualization, there are additional features exposed by the host system, which allow moving costly operations from the guest environment (virtualized) to the host system (native). This requires changes on the guest system to be ported to those para-APIs specific for the hypervisor in use.

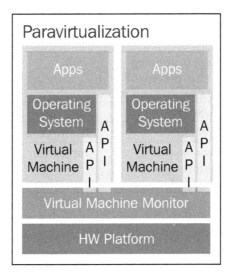

On the other hand, these costly operations should be less costly if executed on the native system compared to execution in a virtual environment.

In terms of security, since there are some resources that are used by multiple machines, it would be easier to cause a hypervisor breakout or to attack another machine without causing a hypervisor breakout first.

Good examples of paravirtualization are Xen and VMware.

Partial virtualization

In partial virtualization, you can find some components that are managed as if in a fully virtualized environment and some that are managed as if in a paravirtualization environment.

Comparison of virtualization levels

The various kinds of virtualization are different from each other. The most important differences are as follows:

Aspect	Full virtualization	Paravirtualization	Partial virtualization
Driver	Native	Ad-hoc	Some Native some Ad-hoc
Performance	High (if running on hardware with specific instructions)	High	High
Security	Maximum	High	High
Compatibility	Every OS	Mostly Linux	Mostly Linux
Different architecture between guest and host	Possible (with performance decrease)	Impossible	Impossible

Since there is no ultimate solution that fits all needs, it's important to understand exactly what the requirements are to make the right decision.

Hypervisors

OpenStack Nova supports multiple hypervisors. Some of them have more functions usable through OpenStack, while others have less.

Kernel-based Virtual Machine

Kernel-based Virtual Machine (KVM) is a hypervisor that is currently part of the Linux Kernel since Linux 2.6.20 released in February 2007. Initially, it was available only for x86 platforms, but today a large number of platforms are supported, including ARM, IA-64, PowerPC, and S/390.

By default, KVM works in a fully virtualized environment, while with some guests, it is possible to use paravirtualization for improved performance.

Being part of the core Linux Kernel is one of the biggest advantages of KVM, since it's often updated and very widely used. Other advantages are its low **Total Cost of Operation (TCO)**, which is calculated to be between 30 percent to 90 percent cheaper than the other leading platforms (open source and proprietary), due to its high efficiency and no license cost.

This comes at the cost of not always having all features those other platforms support. However, KVM has all main virtualization features and a lot of additional features, and its feature list is getting longer with every release, making it a very active project.

KVM is also known for its high security, since it integrates with **Security Enhanced Linux (SELinux)** in the EL distributions (for example, Red Hat Enterprise Linux and CentOS).

Red Hat Enterprise Virtualization (RHEV) is based on KVM to provide virtual machines.

Xen

Xen was created at the University of Cambridge in 2003. Initially, XenSource, Inc. was created to cope with the needs of Xen and its customers. Then, in 2007, the company was acquired by Citrix, which now is the main contributor to the project. In 2013, Citrix announced that the Xen Project would be controlled by the Linux Foundation as a collaborative project.

Since the release of Linux 3.0 in 2011, some components of Xen have been included in the Kernel, so those systems can work as Xen guests in a paravirtualized environment without any modifications.

Xen is probably the most used solution for public clouds; in fact, Amazon EC2, cloud.com, IBM SoftLayer, Liquid Web, Fujitsu Global Cloud Platform, Linode, OrionVM, and Rackspace Cloud use it.

One of the reasons that so many companies use Xen is because it supports five different levels of virtualizations:

- **Hardware Virtual Machine (HVM)**
- **Hardware Virtual Machine with Paravirtualization drivers (HVM + PV drivers)**
- **PVHVM**
- **PVH**
- **Paravirtualized PV**

Item	Xen HVM	Xen PV
Physical CPUs	4,095	4,095
Physical RAM	16 TB	16 TB
Virtual CPU per guest	256	512
RAM per guest	1 TB	512 GB

VMware ESXi

VMware, Inc. was founded in 1998, and in 2004, it was bought by EMC Corporation. In 2007, 15 percent of its shares were made public on NYSE. VMware specializes in virtualization technologies, and it is probably the biggest provider of software for such services.

VMware ESXi started as a compact version of **VMware Elastic Sky X** (**ESX**). Since 2012, no new versions of VMware ESX have been released, and today, VMware ESXi is the VMware standard for servers. Unlike XEN and KVM, VMware ESXi is only available with a commercial license.

Like all the other hypervisors, VMware ESXi has its limitations. Its main limitations are as follows:

Item	Host	Guest
Maximum RAM	6 TB (on certified systems is 12 TB)	4 TB
Maximum processors	480	128
Maximum number of guests	1024	-

Hyper-V

Hyper-V was presented by Microsoft in Windows Server 2008, and it is available in all versions of Windows Server since 2008. Hyper-V uses paravirtualization to provide virtual machines.

Currently, only a small number of operating systems are available as Hyper-V guests, and only Microsoft operating systems are available as Hyper-V hosts.

Baremetal

OpenStack Nova also uses real servers as if they were virtualized guest machines. Users can be given real server and virtual machines as guest machines in a transparent manner. This allows you to use real machines for some tasks you already know will be heavy loaded and could have an impact the performance of your cluster.

Until the Icehouse release, it was possible to use baremetal machine by using the Nova-Baremetal backend, but since the Juno release, the current right way is by using OpenStack Ironic.

This option can even be considered for security reasons, since if you use Ironic (or Nova-Baremetal) you'll end up having a single virtual machine on the physical server. This means that this server will not share computing resources (RAM, CPU, and so on) with other virtual machines, preventing any consequence of a possible hypervisor breakout.

 For machines that require a special level of security, using a baremetal hypervisor (Nova-Baremetal or OpenStack Ironic) could be a good option.

Another advantage of this kind of setup is the possibility of using specific hardware, such as **Hardware Security Module (HSM)**, graphic cards, or physical cards.

On the other side of the coin, OpenStack Ironic has fewer features than the other hypervisors, which can be very useful in some environments, such as the possibility of attaching and unattaching a block storage device via OpenStack; the ability to migrate the machine from a physical server to another; and the ability to use VLANs. Some of these features have not yet been developed in OpenStack Ironic due to the newness of the project, while one physical server to another.

If you are evaluating Baremetal options, you'll have to create procedures to sanitize the nodes before their reuse: you will have to make sure that the previous tenant data has been safely removed; on the other hand, you will have to make sure that the previous tenant has not tampered or compromised the hardware in any way.

 Baremetal nodes need to be sanitized before they can be used for a different machine.

Containers

In recent years, a new technology has been introduced: the container system, such as **Linux Containers (LXC)** and **Docker**. From a technical standpoint, these technologies are placed between high-level virtualization (such as **OpenVZ**) and a **chroot**. However, LXC and Docker are different from these virtualization technologies on the interaction level because the containers have high-level API to provide high levels of encapsulation and isolation.

This allows deploying a container independently from the underlying system with minimal effort. For instance, you could create a container with a website and deploy it on different infrastructures, such as OpenStack, Amazon AWS, CoreOS, and Google Cloud Platform without modifying it. This gives you the obvious advantage of portability but also an additional advantage of having a hybrid infrastructure that uses resources offered by different providers, benefiting from the pricing, the scalability, and other aspects.

OpenStack Nova supports multiple containers, such as LXC, Docker, and Kubernetes. Containers are becoming so important in the IT world and in OpenStack that a group of people in the OpenStack world is working on a new project (OpenStack Magnum) to create a separate module of OpenStack to managed containers. OpenStack Magnum will probably arrive in the official OpenStack distribution in the 2016 release. Until then, OpenStack Nova will service running containers.

Since this kind of deployment is newer than that of classic hypervisors, it is more probable for this kind of deployment to have some security bugs.

 To grant maximum security in a containers environment, you should always use unprivileged containers and add an extra security layers, such as **AppArmor**, **SELinux**, or **GRSEC**.

Docker

Docker is probably the single most popular container service. It was released as an open source project in March 2013 by dotCloud, Inc., and since then, major players like Red Hat and Microsoft have started collaborating with it.

From a security standpoint, Docker can be considered very safe even if it's a new technology, since it does not manage a majority of its security features. Instead, these are demanded to the Linux Kernel, which uses well-tested modules, such as **cgroups**, **SELinux**, and **AppArmor**.

Linux Containers

Linux Containers (**LXC**) is a container management system that was integrated in the Linux Kernel 2.6.24 in August 2008. Like Docker, it uses many kernel modules, such as cgroups, SELinux, and AppArmor.

As for security, there have been real-world cases where users were able to escape from LXC limits, with Linux Kernels older than 3.8 and without proper patching. Since LXC 1.0, thanks to architectural redesigning and the use of unprivileged containers, no more container escape has been possible in properly configured environments.

Criteria for choosing a hypervisor

There are multiple factors that must be considered when you choose which hypervisor to use. The majority of these criteria have security issues, and as you'll see, there is no universal answer that will fit any environment, but each single company will have to find the best tool for its needs. Also, all these hypervisors have an amazing speed of evolution, so hypervisors that are not ready for production now could be ready for production in a few months.

Team expertise

I believe that a very important part of the hypervisor choice has to be based on your staff expertise. There are cases where it makes sense to deploy a hypervisor where none of your staff has any kind of expertise, and this could also be your situation. The downside of this is that your staff will need to study the hypervisor well before it can go into a production environment.

I would say that this could be considered the economical part of the decision; in fact, it affects mainly that part.

Never put in production a hypervisor (as any other piece of software) unless you have someone in your team that is very skilled with it. If you fail to do so, you'll risk having huge security and availability problems.

Please remember, however, that having only a single staff member who knows how to use a software well is dangerous, because if this person is unavailable for some reason, a huge amount of knowhow on that particular software will be unavailable. Also, in case of particular complex systems, such as a hypervisor or an operative system, you'll need to define multiple roles (such as a system administrator and a security administrator), which will require at least two people with an advanced skill set in the use of that technology. In the segregation of duties, it will not be possible to assign both roles to the same person.

Product or project maturity

The maturity of a project should be a critical point in making the decision to put software in a production environment. As you can imagine, putting immature software in production can result in unexpected bugs or instability. Another good reason not to do so is for security. Immature software can contain huge security flaws that can give access to your system to people with malicious intentions. A single unsecure software can compromise the security of your whole system.

In my opinion, there are two aspects of project maturity:

- Source code maturity
- Ecosystem maturity

Source code maturity is merely about the code:

- Is the code secure?
- How well is the code documented?
- How many warning and errors occur on compilation (if it is compiled software)?

Ecosystem maturity is about the people who use the code:

- Is there an active community?
- Is it easy to find people with good knowledge of the software?
- Does the core developer respond to user questions?

Is there an official site and/or an official community?

- Are there examples of companies already using this software in production? How big are the known deployments?
- Are there any collection of best practices?
- Are there any architecture references?
- Is it a developer that publishes the source when a new version is ready or is the software developed in an open source way?
- Is there any company that will sell you commercial support?

Clearly, there are some areas of overlap, for instance:

- Has the code a lot of open bugs?
- How often are new versions released?

Since we are talking about hypervisors for OpenStack, I would also question myself on how good the specific hypervisor supported by OpenStack is:

- Do the hypervisors have OpenStack integration for the features you need?

Certifications and attestations

Another important thing to consider is certification. A majority of hypervisors have been verified and certified by third parties due to the highly critical nature of this software.

Certification does not guarantee that everything will always work properly, but at least will be proof that the software has been vetted by a third party. Also, certifications can be a requirement of your company policy or management.

One of the most acknowledged certifications is **Common Criteria**. Since July 2002, all United States government agencies are required to exclusively use software that have been Common Criteria certified, and many other companies require the same.

A big difference between the Common Criteria certification and many other certifications is that the process evaluates how the technologies have been developed. An important part of the process is the evaluation of the security of the code management system and of the distribution of the binaries themselves.

Features and performance

As you can imagine, different hypervisors have different features and performance. In some cases, a hypervisor will perform better than another will. If you have some very specific feature requirements or particular loads that would perform much better on a particular hypervisor compared to another, this could be a good basis to make the decision to use the hypervisor.

An example of an important feature that KVM provides that the other hypervisors don't is the integration with SELinux. In fact, by default, if SELinux is enabled, every KVM machine obtains its own security context.

Hardware concerns

There are some features that different hypervisors implement in different ways. Often, different hypervisors decide to use (or not use) hardware technologies such as **VT-d** and **AMD-Vi** to secure PCI pass-through.

Each hypervisor has its **Hardware Compatibility List** (**HCL**), which is important to analyze during the hypervisory decision process. Based on the hardware you own or you decide to buy, different hypervisors can use different sets of technologies.

Hypervisor memory optimization

Many times, you'll run multiple virtual machines that are created in very similar ways. For instance, let's suppose you have 100 guest machines on a cluster, and of these, you have 60 RHEL6, 20 RHEL7, and 20 machines with different OS and/or versions. This is a pretty common deployment, since usually, a company tends to use the same Linux distribution and version. In this case, as you can easily imagine, you'll have 60 equal RHEL6 kernels in RAM (plus other 20 of RHEL7). The same will apply to other daemons that will be the same in multiple different machines. All this memory is wasted, since it contains the same data multiple times.

Many hypervisors have the ability to share equal numbers of memory pages between machines. To do so, usually a **Copy On Write** (**COW**) system is used. The downside of this is that the COW mechanism can be vulnerable to side-channel attacks, since the owner of a machine could infer something about another machine state. Due to this, in untrusted environments or in environments with untrusted tenants, it's unsafe to use this kind of optimization.

In case you have some trusted users and some untrusted users, it would make sense to use hypervisor memory optimization only among trusted users. There are multiple ways to do so. The two most common ways include creating different server groups to ensure that only machines in a certain server group are allowed to use hypervisor memory optimization, and creating multiple host groups to be able to physically divide the hosts, ensuring that trusted users use only some of them. Therefore, this requires setting up hosts used only by trusted users to allow hypervisor memory optimization.

 Although hypervisor memory optimization can allow big RAM savings, it can expose your machines to side-channel attacks from an untrusted tenant.

The two major hypervisors that sport this feature are KVM and XEN. KVM has used the **Kernel Samepage Merging (KSM)** module since Linux 2.6.32 to consolidate identical memory pages. XEN, since XenServer 5.6, includes the **Transparent Page Sharing (TPS)** feature to share identical chunks of memory of 4 KB between different machines.

Both KSM and TPS have been proven vulnerable to side-channel attacks.

Additional security features

Since virtualization brings new challenges from a security standpoint, multiple hardening solutions have been implemented by different companies, but not all hypervisors support all hardening solutions. The five major hardening solutions that have been developed are **AppArmor**, **cgroups**, **Intel Trusted Execution Technology (Intel TXT)**, **sVirt**, and **Xen Security Modules (XSM)**. The following table will show you which technologies the different hypervisors support:

Technology	KVM	XEN	ESXi	Hyper-V
XSM		Yes		
AppArmor	Yes			
cgroups	Yes			
sVirt	Yes			
Intel TXT	Yes	Yes	Yes	

Hardening the hardware management

There are two aspects of hardware management: one involves providing physical hardware to virtual machines securely, while the other involves providing virtual hardware securely.

Physical hardware – PCI passthrough

As the IT world is moving towards a more complete virtualization of the system, the need to use more than the classic CPU, RAM, storage and networking in virtualized environments is becoming more and more common. One of the most common scenarios is the need to access from virtual machines to video cards and GPUs for high performance **Compute Unified Device Architecture (CUDA)**. A lot of hypervisors give you this kind of capability, but it brings two possible security risks.

Direct Memory Access (DMA) is a feature that allows many hardware devices to access the machine RAM directly and without any control. This feature allows the device to have a huge latency reduction in the read and write operations, so many low-latency devices, such as video cards and SCSI controllers use it. If an instance has free access to a device that has free access to the host RAM, it will be possible for that instance to read the host RAM and all the running instances on that host. To solve this, an **Input/Output Memory Management Unit (IOMMU)** has been integrated in CPUs. AMD's **I/O Virtualization Technology (AMD-Vi)** and Intel's **Virtualization Technology for Directed I/O (VT-d)** are both implementations of IOMMU.

 If you are going to allow instances to access hardware directly, be sure that your CPU and hypervisor allow you to use an IOMMU system.

The other risk you can face is hardware infection. Some hardware pieces allow the software to edit or flash the firmware. If this is the case, an instance could mess with the firmware, adding some malicious code to obtain data or access to machines that will use the same hardware after that moment. For this kind of scenario, there is no one-size-fits-all solution. A solution that would be easy to implement is to reflash the firmware after every use. This solution is not usable in the real world because the firmware chips have a limited amount of possible writes. This would make the hardware life pretty short. A way to make the hardware life longer is to flash the firmware only if it has changed. To identify if the firmware has been tampered with, the **Trusted Platform Module (TPM)** could help to check that if the signature and the checksum of the firmware is valid.

Due to the security criticalities we have just seen, my advice is to keep the PCI passthrough disabled by default, and to enable it only in the instances where its really needed. A good way to do so is by creating different flavors of guest with and without PCI passthrough and keeping the ones with the PCI passthrough enabled privately only for the specific projects that need it.

Virtual hardware with Quick Emulator

There are cases where software expects to find a certain kind of hardware but it does not require it to be high performing. Another situation that can bring you to this approach is if you need hardware that you don't have. Typical examples of these cases are software that require floppy disks, CDs, or specific hardware, since they are legacy software written in assembly or other similar low-level languages.

The best open source software to provide virtual hardware is **Quick Emulator (QEMU)**. QEMU is advanced software that allows you to virtualize a huge amount of hardware no matter what the real hardware QEMU is running on. This allows it to virtualize different platforms from the one it's running on, so with QEMU, you can create an ARM instance on an Intel node. Even though QEMU code has been heavily improved over the last few years, it still has a lot of low-level code that is hard to write and maintain; so it still has many critical bugs. Historically, the majority of hypervisory breakout cases are connected with QEMU, so extra caution is necessary when dealing with it:

- The first thing to do to reduce the probability of a QEMU exploit on your machine is to reduce the attack surface by not providing any virtual hardware by default and providing it only if needed.

- The second aspect is connected with how you obtain QEMU itself. The easiest way to obtain QEMU is through the package manager of your distribution. All major distribution today ships QEMU compiled in the most secure way possible. Another way to obtain it is by compiling it from sources. In this case, you'll have to take care to use all compiler-hardening options. The security advantage of this method relies on the possibility of disabling the compilation of the code-implementing devices that you don't want to provide to your users. This will decrease the amount of QEMU code running on your machines.

 If you are going to compile QEMU by yourself, create a repository that all your machines access, create, and push the new packages, using it to ensure that all your machines run the same version of each software. This will help you manage and debug your cloud and will allow you to push security updates to all nodes in a very short amount of time.

No matter how you obtained QEMU, it can happen that somehow an attacker successfully violates it. To minimize the consequences of this, you need to have a **Mandatory Access Control (MAC)** system in place (I suggest using SELinux) and use a different security context for each virtual machine. As mentioned earlier, to do a very inexpensive way is to use the KVM hypervisor, since it will do so by default.

sVirt – SELinux and virtualization

Security-Enhanced Linux (**SELinux**) is a Linux module that was originally developed by the United States National Security Agency (NSA) in 1998, and that has been part of the main Linux Kernel since 2.6.0 since August 2003. Since then, Red Hat, Secure Computing Corporation, and many other companies have helped improve it.

SELinux implements MAC architecture directly in the Linux Kernel, limiting user access to all resources: files, network devices, or any other kind of resource. SELinux integrates with the standard UNIX DAC system but works differently. In fact, it does not recognize root as a privileged user, neither does it accept any shortcoming that has been built to help pass security limitations in the UNIX DAC (for example, the `setuid` and the `setgid` systems). To identify who can do what, each resource has an SELinux context that looks like this:

```
system_u:object_r:httpd_sys_content_t:s0
```

It is composed of a **user** (`system_u`), a **role** (`object_r`), a **type** (`httpd_sys_content_t`), and a **level** (`s0`). The level can be simple (like `s0`) if the SELinux is run in targeted mode, or more complex (like `s0-s0:c0.c1023`) if SELinux is run in **Multi-Level Security** (**MLS**) mode.

Since 2002, **Secure Virtualization** (**sVirt**) has been developed to bring the security of SELinux to hypervisors to isolate the instances. The sVirt implementation found in OpenStack has two major goals:

- Protecting the host from a malicious instance
- Protecting the other instances from a malicious instance

To do so, each VM created using KVM runs with a different SELinux label, so it creates a fence around each VM, creating a specific category set for each one.

Since SELinux does not support infinite categories, if you use SELinux, only 524,288 instances can be run concurrently on each physical node. This should not be an issue in the majority of cases, but it is better to be aware of it.

Since SELinux is very flexible, and it makes sense to keep it in the strictest way that allows your system to do exactly what it is supposed to do and nothing more, many distributions ship it with the Booleans that allow you to enable or disable whole sets of allowances with a single command. Examples of SELinux Booleans that deal with sVirt are:

- `virt_use_common`: This manages the ability of the instances to use serial/parallel communication ports
- `virt_use_fusefs`: This manages the ability of the instances to use FUSE-mounted filesystems
- `virt_use_nfs`: This manages the ability of the instances to use NFS mounted filesystems
- `virt_use_samba`: This manages the ability of the instances to use CIFS mounted filesystems
- `virt_use_sanlock`: This manages the ability of the instances to interact with the sanlock
- `virt_use_sysfs`: This manages the ability of the instances to manage device configuration (PCI)
- `virt_use_usb`: This manages the ability of the instances to use USB devices
- `virt_use_xserver`: manages the ability of the instances to interact with the X Window System

Even if SELinux is not the only way to harden OpenStack, I've found out that it provides the best isolation and, therefore, the best security. It is also very well integrated with KVM, as both are part of the Linux Kernel.

Hardening the host operative system

There are many paths to harden a given operating system deployment. The specifics on these steps are outside of the scope of this book. I recommend referring to a hardening guide specific to your operating system.

For example, the **Security Technical Implementation Guides** (**STIG**) and the NSA guides are useful starting places along with the OS vendor documentation.

Summary

In this chapter, we covered the compute component from a security standpoint. Securing OpenStack Nova is a critical part of securing the whole infrastructure and requires special caution since the biggest part is executed by making wise choices during the initial design of the cloud itself.

In this book, we have covered several theoretical concepts about how technologies used by OpenStack work, to understand better how to secure them; this is necessary to have a better understanding of how, what, and why the systems you are going to manage are structured. This, in turn, is necessary for security, since exploit and hardening methods change every day, while the ideas behind them tend to be less volatile. We also saw how to harden various parts of OpenStack to ensure that your system will resist all common attacks.

Index

Symbol

0-day attack 32

A

access control
  about 1
  Discretionary Access Control (DAC) 1
  Mandatory Access Control (MAC) 2
  Role-based Access Control (RBAC) 2
Address Resolution Protocol (ARP)
    spoofing 46
Advanced Encryption Standard (AES) 67
Advanced Persistent DoS (APDoS) 31
Advanced Persistent Threat 33
Amazon CloudFormation 39
Amazon CloudWatch 39
Amazon Elastic Block Store (EBS) 39
Amazon Elastic Compute Cloud (EC2) 36
Amazon Elastic MapReduce (EMR) 40
Amazon Machine Image (AMI) 37
Amazon Relational Database
    Service (RDS) 40
Amazon Route 41, 53
Amazon Simple Notification
    Service (SNS) 41
Amazon Simple Queue Service (SQS) 41
Amazon Simple Storage Service (S3) 36
Amazon Web Services (AWS) 38
AMD-Vi 124
Apache HTTPd
  about 79, 80
  configuring 95, 96

APIs
  redundant environment,
    designing for 77-79
AppArmor 120, 125
application firewall 56
application layer, Open Systems
    Interconnection (OSI) model 52
asymmetric encryption
  about 67
  Diffie-Hellman 68
  Elliptic Curve Cryptography (ECC) 69
  RSA algorithm 69
  versus symmetric encryption 70
attackers
  about 30
  automated attacks/script kiddies 30
  highly capable groups 30
  intelligence agencies/services 30
  motivated individuals 30
  organized hackers 30
attacks
  0-day 32
  about 30
  Advanced Persistent Threat 33
  Automated exploitation tools 33
  Brute force 33
  Denial of Service (DoS) 31, 32
  Hypervisor breakout 35
  ISP intercept 34
  social engineering 35
  supply chain attack 34
authentication
  about 83, 84
  behavioral characteristics 87

additional security features 125
attestations 123
certifications 123
features 123
hardware concerns 124
hypervisor memory optimization 124
performance 123
team expertise 121

D

data center security
about 11
authorization points, securing 13
blueprints 15
cameras 14
castle-like structure, implementing 12
data center, in office 15
employees, defending 13
location, selecting 11
low profile, keeping 13
power of redundancy 14
support systems, defending 13
Data Encryption Standard (DES) 67
data link layer, Open Systems
Interconnection (OSI) model
about 45, 46
Address Resolution Protocol (ARP)
    spoofing 46
CAM table overflow attack 47
Cisco Discovery Protocol (CDP) attacks 48
Dynamic Host Configuration Protocol
    (DHCP) starvation attack 47
MAC flooding attack 47
Spanning Tree Protocol (STP) attacks 48, 49
Virtual LAN (VLAN) attacks 49
Defense in depth 10
Denial of Service (DoS) attack
about 31
buffer overflow attacks 32
smurf attacks 32
SYN Flood attacks 32
teardrop attacks 32
viruses/worms 32
Designate 41
Diffie-Hellman protocol
generator (g) 68

parameter (p) 68
Direct Memory Access (DMA) 126
discrete logarithm problem 69
Discretionary Access Control (DAC) 89
Docker 119, 120
Domain Name System (DNS) 52
DoS 5
DoS Defense System (DDS) 31
DreamObject Cloud Store 105
Dual Elliptic Curve Deterministic Random
**   Bit Generation (Dual_EC_DRBG) 70**
Dynamic Host Configuration Protocol
**   (DHCP) 46**
Dynamic Host Configuration Protocol
**   (DHCP) starvation attack 47**

E

Economic Denial of Sustainability (EDoS) 6
Edwards-curve Digital Signature Algorithm
**   (EdDSA) 69**
Elliptic Curve Cryptography (ECC) 69
Elliptic Curve Diffie-Hellman (ECDH) 69
Elliptic Curve Digital Signature Algorithm
**   (ECDSA) 69**
encryption security 64
Enhanced Interior Gateway Routing
**   Protocol (EIGRP) 50**
examples of SELinux Booleans, dealing
**   with sVirt**
virt_use_common 129
virt_use_fusefs 129
virt_use_nfs 129
virt_use_samba 129
virt_use_sanlock 129
virt_use_sysfs 129
virt_use_usb 129
virt_use_xserver 129
Extended Validation (EV) 75

F

Federated identity 90, 91
Fiber Channel (FC) 100
Fiber Channel over Ethernet (FCoE) 100
files, on filesystems
drawbacks 17

Thank you for buying
OpenStack Cloud Security

About Packt Publishing

Packt, pronounced 'packed', published its first book, *Mastering phpMyAdmin for Effective MySQL Management*, in April 2004, and subsequently continued to specialize in publishing highly focused books on specific technologies and solutions.

Our books and publications share the experiences of your fellow IT professionals in adapting and customizing today's systems, applications, and frameworks. Our solution-based books give you the knowledge and power to customize the software and technologies you're using to get the job done. Packt books are more specific and less general than the IT books you have seen in the past. Our unique business model allows us to bring you more focused information, giving you more of what you need to know, and less of what you don't.

Packt is a modern yet unique publishing company that focuses on producing quality, cutting-edge books for communities of developers, administrators, and newbies alike. For more information, please visit our website at www.packtpub.com.

About Packt Open Source

In 2010, Packt launched two new brands, Packt Open Source and Packt Enterprise, in order to continue its focus on specialization. This book is part of the Packt Open Source brand, home to books published on software built around open source licenses, and offering information to anybody from advanced developers to budding web designers. The Open Source brand also runs Packt's Open Source Royalty Scheme, by which Packt gives a royalty to each open source project about whose software a book is sold.

Writing for Packt

We welcome all inquiries from people who are interested in authoring. Book proposals should be sent to author@packtpub.com. If your book idea is still at an early stage and you would like to discuss it first before writing a formal book proposal, then please contact us; one of our commissioning editors will get in touch with you.

We're not just looking for published authors; if you have strong technical skills but no writing experience, our experienced editors can help you develop a writing career, or simply get some additional reward for your expertise.

Learning OpenStack Networking (Neutron)

ISBN: 978-1-78398-330-8 Paperback: 300 pages

Architect and build a network infrastructure for your cloud using OpenStack Neutron networking

1. Build a virtual switching infrastructure for virtual machines using the Open vSwitch or Linux Bridge plugins.

2. Create networks and software routers that connect virtual machines to the Internet using built-in Linux networking features.

3. Scale your application using Neutron's load-balancing-as-a-service feature using the haproxy plugin.

OpenStack Essentials

ISBN: 978-1-78398-708-5 Paperback: 182 pages

Demystify the cloud by building your own private OpenStack cloud

1. Set up a powerful cloud platform using OpenStack.

2. Learn about the components of OpenStack and how they interact with each other.

3. Follow a step-by-step process that exposes the inner details of an OpenStack cluster.

Please check **www.PacktPub.com** for information on our titles

Implementing Cloud Storage with OpenStack Swift

ISBN: 978-1-78216-805-8   Paperback: 140 pages

Design, implement, and successfully manage your own cloud storage cluster using the popular OpenStack Swift software

1. Learn about the fundamentals of cloud storage using OpenStack Swift.

2. Explore how to install and manage OpenStack Swift along with various hardware and tuning options.

3. Perform data transfer and management using REST APIs.

OpenStack Cloud Computing Cookbook

ISBN: 978-1-84951-732-4   Paperback: 318 pages

Over 100 recipes to successfully set up and manage your OpenStack cloud environments with complete coverage of Nova, Swift, Keystone, Glance, and Horizon

1. Learn how to install and configure all the core components of OpenStack to run an environment that can be managed and operated just like AWS or Rackspace.

2. Master the complete private cloud stack from scaling out compute resources to managing swift services for highly redundant, highly available storage.

Please check **www.PacktPub.com** for information on our titles

www.ingramcontent.com/pod-product-compliance
Lightning Source LLC
Chambersburg PA
CBHW060144060326
40690CB00018B/3972